SHADOW WORK PUBLISHING

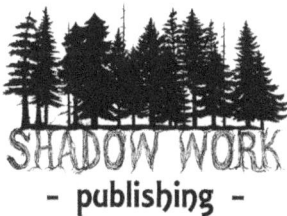

SHADOW WORK
- publishing -

Copyright © 2025 by Duncan Ralston
All rights reserved.

ISBN: 978-1988819631

ALSO BY DUNCAN RALSTON

SHOOT

PORTRAIT OF A PORNOGRAPHER

THE LONELY MOTEL
BOOK FOUR

DUNCAN RALSTON

YOU FEEL LIKE

you've been here before, don't you?

Take a look around. See the stained carpet, redder than an orange but more orange than blood. The off-white walls and ceiling, stained in places where stains like that just don't seem possible. The faux silk bedspread, a deeper red than the carpet, almost the color of a Valentine's heart. The drapes that match the bed.

It's just like any other roadside motel you might find on your way from one place to the next, never a destination, always passing through, only it's not at all like any of those places.

You can *feel* that, just by looking at it.

If you saw it on the road ahead, you might just hit the gas to pass it a little quicker. You might even feel a strange urge to hold your breath, like driving past a cemetery when you were a little kid. If you're bold you might consider slowing down, when there's emergency lights flashing and sirens blaring in the lot, like a rubbernecker driving past an accident.

But you'd never stop.

You'd never pull into the lot.

You'd never, God forbid, rent a room for an hour. Or a night.

Not here.

Maybe, looking up at that sign on the roof, the one that says *LONELY* in big red-orange neon letters, you can almost imagine you've been inside. Maybe the *Vacancy* sign even looks familiar. The threadbare drapes and bent metal blinds through the grimy window panes.

But you know you *haven't* been here.

It's got to be déjà vu.

The truth is simpler: you've probably just seen too much porn. Or maybe you've seen that one video, the one that was supposed to be for a few select high-paying clients and somehow got shared all over the 'net. The one with the guy getting his head shoved—

You've seen it. Of course you have. I can tell by the look on your face.

You know, I must've shot a hundred videos in this place but *that's* the one most people will remember me by. They'll put it on my tombstone: "Here lies Chuck P, director of the *Woman Gives Birth to Grown Man* video."

I know of at least a half dozen other producers who've made films here too, but none of them ever made it as big as me. The Lonely Motel is where I got my start. It got me where I am today. We have a... a *special relationship*, I guess you could say. And whether you stay for an hour or for a night, it *changes* you.

You may not think a place can change someone. But believe me: if you spend enough time here, it will. You may not even feel it yourself, but other people will start to notice.

"Something's different..." they'll say next time they

see you, with a funny look like you stepped in something that stinks. And you'll laugh and say, "I dunno," but you'll know.

Trust me. *You'll know.*

But you called me here to talk about me and my career, not listen to sinister ramblings about some place you recognize but never been before. About Powerplay and Bespoke and all that.

Well, if these walls could talk. That's what people say, isn't it? Those stains on the carpet I mentioned, the ceiling—some of them I've filmed myself. Depending on which room, I could probably tell you the origin of each one, like your teacher in third grade naming the constellations. Only these stars have the names of expensive car brands. Or Candy. Or Vixen.

And now that you're actually inside, it doesn't seem so bad, does it? You can kind of pretend it's normal. *Almost.*

That's how it was for me too, when I first came to the Lonely. Shit, I was still just a kid back then. Had to have been... almost twenty-six years ago? Time flies when you're watching people fuck for a living, I guess.

Oh, right. I know I told you on the phone, but just so we're clear: I'm not gonna talk about *that*. This is not about *that*, got it? This isn't going to be a tear-soaked confession, if that's what you're looking for.

I've got nothing to confess, first of all. I am not responsible for what happened, and *I am not going to talk about it.*

Period.

No, we can talk about the so-called "Chuck P. Curse." It's bullshit, you know. Of course it is. But we can talk about it. In fact, just about every bad thing that happened in my twenty-six-year career in porn, I guess it'd be easy enough to fit this "curse" narrative. If I'm honest, I might've even believed in it myself for a while there.

Now? I dunno. I'll let you decide for yourself when we're all finished here.

So where should I start? The "day and hour of my birth," like *David Copperfield*? Nah, that wouldn't be right. My *rebirth*, that's what you want to hear about. How I transformed from a mild-mannered youth to Chuck P., porn mogul extraordinaire.

My real name? What is it they say... names and places are the product of the author's imagination or used fictitiously?

Chuck P. is my stage name, yeah, but it's also what it says on my ID. I had it changed legally to Chuck Power, that's right. So that's my real name as far as anyone should be concerned.

I'm the creator and CEO of Bespoke.com, the multimillion dollar adult entertainment subscription service, and formerly the Bespoke app, which AVN called the "gamification of porn," as well as the director/producer of hundreds of adult films, including *Inside Tammy Rivers*, *I Am Curious (Red)* and *Brown Eyes Wide Open*.

What else? I dunno, you called me.

I *understand* that, but anything pertaining to that situation is off the table. You agreed on that with my lawyer, and I'll walk right now if you ask me about it again. I'm fucking serious, okay? *I'm. Not. Going. To talk about it*.

How I got into the business? Great. That I can do.

I've done a fair amount of interviews over the years, in front and behind the camera, so I know the ropes. In video interviews they ask to use the question in the answer, so I'll probably end up doing that a lot, despite this being for print. I hope that's not too distracting or annoying for your readers.

Okay, great.

So for reference, before I tell you how I got into the business: I always had pull with the ladies, even when I was a kid. Ask anyone who knew me back in the day, they'll tell you. Always had a girl on my arm, even brought two dates to prom. Legend has it I took both their virginities that night, right in this very hotel.

No, of course I didn't. Circumstances prevented it even if I *did* want to. But they were nice enough to play along.

They were beards, yeah. Good ones too. I used to be your stereotypical closeted gay boy. Still am. Gay, I mean. Not in the closet, obviously. I think it's pretty well known in the industry at this point, though I did try to keep it secret for a while in the late '90s and early 2000s. And I'm definitely not a *boy* anymore. Eighteen-year-old me would've died to learn he'd become a silver fox with a receding hairline by his early forties, but there you have it.

And I guess I wasn't technically in the closet either. I was *on the downlow*, as they say. Imagine me playing straight—not gonna happen, right? I knew who I am from a very young age, but I wasn't about to advertise that at a very straight high school in the late-'90s, when everything dumb was "gay," and anyone showing a little bit of sensitivity or emotion aside from getting pissed off was a "fag."

But yeah, I always had what we use to call "pull." And I had a ton of straight friends always wanting to go to the rippers when they couldn't score at whatever club we were at. Though I gotta say, I was a pretty damned good wingman, so it was a rare night at least one of my guy friends didn't go home with a lady, or what we used to call "talent."

That's right, we'd go to the Canadian Ballet. I guess you passed it on your way here, huh? The Ballet was our go-to spot, though it was even sleazier back then. None of the showcases they've put on now, or the specialty shows. No Poncho Night or Thanksgiving Special.

Oh, you *gotta* check out Poncho Night. You ever been on the Behind the Falls thing at Niagara? It's like that, only with a stripper. It sounds gross, I know, but it'll change your whole outlook on life, hand on heart.

Anyway, back then the Ballet was a hole-in-the-wall where you could pay fifty bucks to get your dick sucked in the VIP room, or a couple hundred to fuck at one of the nearby motels.

Just so happened the Lonely Motel was the closest and cheapest, and it already had a pretty bad reputation even then. It was a wonder our folks let us hold the after-prom here. Best we figured was the rumors must've skipped a generation, but that couldn't be right 'cause we'd all heard the stories from our big brothers or pervy uncles or whoever. So the Lonely Motel was a shithole, but it was also the kind of place where bad things seemed to always happen. Like all those little kid fingers they found in the tub drain in the '70s or '80s, left behind by that serial killer? Yeah, we really should've figured we were in for a bad time on prom night, but we all just wanted to get blitzed and maybe get laid in the afterglow of five long, mainly miserable years of secondary education.

Since I was still on the downlow, I wasn't getting off in the VIP or here at the Lonely, at least not with any working girls. By then I'd already figured out getting sucked off by someone of the female persuasion wasn't gonna do it for me unless I had my eyes shut, trying real hard to imagine some Adonis with a fuzzy teenage mustache in tight white baseball pants, or a few of the guys on the swim team with their sleek, hairless muscles. Or Christopher Meloni from *Oz*. I know he was a fucking scumbag in that series but he was sexy as fuck.

Oh, you *have* to watch it. *It's not TV, it's HBO.* That's what their ads used to say.

So anyway, I obviously wasn't getting my rocks off in the VIP at the Ballet or here at the Lonely. What I *was* doing was "learning the craft." I was in a communications class in my last two years and I wanted to go to film school, so I was kinda like that weird kid from *American Beauty*, bringing my video camera everywhere I went. You're probably too young to remember, but it wasn't like these days, everyone's got a camera in their pocket on their phones. This was *conspicuous* as hell. I had a camcorder just about the size of a brick.

Oh you had one? What make? Nice, that's a decent camera. I had the Sony Handycam Vision, the 8-mill not the Hi8. Wasn't high quality but it got the job done. And nobody back in those days gave a fuck about low-quality video. Guys were just happy to get what they got. Shit, most of the guys I grew up with jacked off to scrambled porn when they were kids!

Damn, you're making me feel old here.

So in the '80s they used to have porn channels on satellite—Skinemax, Spice Network, the Playboy Channel—but they were locked unless you paid extra. Yeah, kinda like subscriptions today, only instead of a paywall or whatever you could still sort of see these channels even though the picture was all distorted. You never knew if you were looking at an elbow or a boob, but the moans always came through loud and clear, and if you had a good imagination you could sometimes get off on it like a few of my friends did.

No, the Canadian Ballet wouldn't let me bring my camera in, but off-premises, like at the Lonely, I could get these women to tell me their deepest, darkest secrets just by telling them I was making a documentary about the sex industry, that I'd cover over their faces in the final production if they wanted me to. You know, to protect their identities and all that, since it's illegal to perform sex acts for cash in the state of New York, even though if you do it in front of a camera it's perfectly fine. Go figure.

So that's what I was doing while the boys were busting their nuts in the other rooms. Learning about the sex industry, and earning the trust of these women, all under the guise of "making a documentary." You'd be surprised what you can get away with posing as an independent filmmaker. Or a photographer. Or a writer, I guess, like you.

People open up to you when they think you could make them famous. Give you their trust. Share their secrets. Their bodies sometimes too, if that's your game and you say the right things. Which I guess it was for me, even if I wasn't into their bodies for my own personal gratification.

Reality TV producers, they turned that trick into a multibillion-dollar industry. So did porn producers. That's why you had guys like BangBus and Filthy Lessons getting huge with Gonzo reality porn around the same time I came up. I guess that makes us contemporaries, but I'd never lump myself in with those scumfucks, especially Filthy Lessons.

So anyway, I spent my last year of high school

making a documentary that'd never see the inside of an edit suite, at least not the ones at school. I watched those tapes on repeat on my computer at home though. Never once got caught by my folks either. How's that for slick?

How did we get into the Ballet? Well, we had great fake IDs but we never had to use em. We didn't exactly look twenty-one either. If I'm honest, back then the Ballet didn't give a fuck about underage drinkers. They've gotten stricter with that in the past decade or so, but the previous owner was a bit of a scumfuck who didn't give two shits if a bunch of teenage boys got an eyeful of titties, so long as they paid the five-bucks cover and ordered two drinks each. Didn't matter if they nursed those same two drinks all night, so long as they didn't harass the staff and kept their paws off the girls. Outside of the VIP anyway. In the champagne room— which at the Canadian Ballet was more of a Mad Dog 20 20 room, if you're not too young to understand the reference—it was anything goes, as long as the girls agreed and you paid them up front.

I made my first sex tape in 1999, when the internet was still taking baby steps. A dancer who called herself Tammy Rivers agreed to star in it with a guy she picked out at the club who had good abs and was eager to fuck. I paid her twice what she'd get for a full-meal deal at the Lonely, plus another hundred bucks on top. Five hundred total.

A full-meal deal is just what it sounds like. That's the whole enchilada, like they used to say. Fucking, sucking, orgasm.

Oh, the guy? I didn't pay him a dime. Didn't have to. He was just happy to get laid. You can't find that video on the internet anymore, by the way. The guy had it scrubbed. He's a senator now, if you believe that. Hand on heart.

Obviously, I was just learning the ropes at the time, so my direction was sloppy and very much on-camera. I was nervous, they were nervous, and it really showed. The fucking was way beyond amateur, even though Tammy'd already banged through all my guy friends at least once and probably half the clientele at the club too. Despite all that, or maybe because of it, that video put my little Powerplay webpage on the map. Most porn was still using condoms back then 'cause this scumfuck motherfucker hid he was HIV-positive for like two years and infected at least four women, probably more. But the fact that Tammy put the condom on this soon-to-be-senator's surprisingly thick, uncut cock with her mouth was pretty damned impressive, especially for an FTV.

FTV? That's industry slang for First Time Video. Those ones are particularly sought-out by certain types of guys. First Time Video, Barely Legal, First Time Anal, etcetera. And they can be gold mines if your girl becomes a big star. Ed Powers—no relation, his name has an S—you know, the *Dirty Debutantes* guy? He built an empire out of those videos. Probably holds the world record for breaking in new girls who wound up household names, if that record doesn't already belong to the Hedgehog, Ron Jeremy.

That FTV with Tammy, not only did it put my little page on the map, Tammy herself blew up huge after that. She was this sweet, innocent-looking blonde chick but she could suck-start a lawnmower, like they say. For guys who didn't know her—you know, didn't know she'd been stripping at the Ballet for two years since she flunked out of high school, and probably fucked half the local high school football teams, and actually had a two-year-old kid waiting for her at home while she was out fucking a stranger on camera—it was like seeing the girl next door turn into an insatiable nympho right in front of their eyes.

She was beautiful, yeah. You know you actually kind of look like her, if I'm honest. Not entirely, maybe it's just the eyes. Or the cheekbones. The chin? Have you ever considered—?

No, you don't look like you're built for *this* industry, I can tell that. I just mean modeling.

No? Well, you could if you wanted to. Got that look, you know? That confidence. It's in the eyes.

As for our soon-to-be-senator, in addition to having a great cock, he lasted surprisingly longer than I expected for a first-timer. I still feel like he might be in the closet, but he did finally come on her face like I told him to, even though I practically had to count him down to it. After he left—he had an algebra quiz the next day or some shit—Tammy and I hung out a bit and got smashed, and she comes up with the bright idea she wants to suck off a beer bottle like Madonna in *Truth or Dare*. Only Tammy being Tammy, she fucked it afterwards, and I'm pretty sure the Material Girl never went that far, at least not on camera.

And that was it: that was the watershed moment for my career. It was—what do you call it? Lightning in a bottle, yeah. Tons of viewers seemed to appreciate that part, the beer-bottle insertion, judging by all the comments I got on the page.

Miller High Life. Yeah, the champagne of beers. So sure, she fucked a beer bottle, but at least it was classy.

Anyway, the page blew up within a week of uploading that first video, so I paid to get a domain name and all that, and of course Girls Gone Wild was huge around that time, so I was accused of riding on their coattails. Fuck those guys though. Bunch of assholes, especially the prick who ran it.

Yeah, I heard there was some documentary about sex abuse allegations? Talk about wild. Scumfucks like that give all of us a bad name.

My own lawsuit came later. Eventually we settled with the soon-to-be-senator, after I incorporated in 2002, and I had to blur his face for the whole thing, which sucked to do since he had a very pretty face, so much that some of my fellow gays even seemed to appreciate the video, despite it being a guy-girl scene without any pegging or any "sissy" stuff. I even had plenty of requests for his info from producers wanting him to do gay-for-pay, little did they know. But that was his first and only video, which made it all the more special. Those rare videos are like finding buried treasure for porn fanatics.

But then the soon-to-be-senator got into politics and came at us with some heavy-hitting lawyers, so we pulled it from the site and he got it scrubbed from the 'net.

By that time we had almost two hundred videos on the site, so it wasn't a huge deal. We were making money hand-over-fist, and I was just glad he didn't sue for cash. I've seen a fair amount of my contemporaries go out of business and file for bankruptcy over the years and I'm still standing, as Elton John would say. I guess I can't credit that video for propelling the senator to his current career, but Tammy Rivers went on to star in dozens of videos after that. She was on Wicked Pictures' roster for a while there. Even won an AVN award for Most

Outrageous Sex Scene before she retired from acting in 2013.

Me? I couldn't have been prouder. And the fact that she never forgot where she got her start really touched my heart. Some of these kids, they act like they were destined for stardom and you were just a stone they stepped on in the path that paved their way. Not Tammy. She invited me to be her date for the ceremony despite being married to a long-time collaborator, but my dumb ass couldn't make it on account of a shoot in Toronto I booked that same weekend. I did end up attending a bunch of them over the years anyway, and I guess you already know I won an AVN myself a few years back for Best Internet Subscription Service with Bespoke.com. And Tammy and I worked together again for over a decade when she came back home.

It's a little early to get into that, isn't it? You want me to jump from my first time right to the pinnacle of my career? Or the pinnacle *so far*, I should say. I don't want to jinx it.

Not that I don't feel like I haven't been jinxed already lately, especially after....

Well, anyway, let's try to do this chronologically. That'll help you keep track of everything as we go. Or I guess as close to chronological as I can. I can be a bit scatterbrained at times, like you haven't already noticed. Going off on tangents is my other hidden talent.

What's the first? Ask my husband.

Actually, don't. He'd probably say something like "always putting the can opener back in the wrong drawer" or "using the shower soap without a wash cloth." You know, just to mess with me. He's like that sometimes.

A wash cloth? I think it's a cultural thing. I just rinse the bar when I'm done, don't you?

Oh, so maybe I *am* the weird one.

So what came next? Well, for about six months or so, after that first video with Tammy, she roped in other girls who wanted their fifteen minutes of fame. We did girl/girl scenes. We did MFMs, that's a threesome with two guys and a girl, what my high school buddies would've called a "devil's threesome." We did DPs, double vaginal, double anal, gangbangs. We did lesbian fisting and self-fisting and some piss play videos—you know, watersports—which did really well in the German and Czech markets. Man, we did everything we could think of just to chase that high from the first one.

And most of them were mildly successful, don't get me wrong. We paid the bills, anyway. But we didn't hit that same high we did with Tammy's FTV until we stumbled onto Marcus Handler.

That's right. We called him that 'cause of that lawyer movie with a young Matt Damon when he was still a *mangenue*, but also for obvious reasons, if you've seen any of his videos.

The man was *obsessed* with making women squirt. Like literally *obsessed*.

That's why we called him—

THE RAINMAKER

So we found Marcus Handler by accident.

Or I guess word of him eventually got around to Tammy, and Tammy brought him to me.

Marcus—that's not his given name, but you can look it up if you're that interested—he was a regular at the Canadian Ballet for a year or so before he caught Tammy's attention. Never drank more than his two beers, after that it was Diet Coke. Always dressed well. Always smelled clean, like sandalwood and citrus with a hint of sweet tobacco. Always wore a black suit with his hair slicked back like he just stepped off the set of *Reservoir Dogs* or some Mafia movie. Real cool cat, aside from his fetish, which would've been okay itself if he didn't suck at it.

Once every payday, he'd pay his two hundred, take one girl after the next over to one of these rooms here at the Lonely and spend the whole time trying to make these poor girls squirt. It got to the point one or two of them would make themselves piss just so he'd give it a rest and let them get back to dancing, even if their legs were bowed from him slamming his middle two fingers on their g-spot like he's the fucking Pinball Wizard.

But somehow he knew it wasn't real. He was practicing. He was honing his craft down to a fine art. The gentle art of making women cream. Or not-so-gentle, in this case.

Even way back then, Marcus became a bit of a legend among the girls. They'd all talk about this guy who was like the Little Engine That Could, except he couldn't. One of them got it in their heads, she must've been reading the book to her kid or some shit, then they all started to think about it when Marcus started punching their secondary fuck-button: *I think he can, I think he can, I think he can*. You know, sort of cheering him on in their heads. 'Cause if he *could* do it that'd be mission accomplished, or so they thought, and they could get back to having mediocre sex with the other patrons.

So they all started trying their hardest to help him along, rather than sitting there or lying there trying not to be bored while the Rainmaker-in-training fingerblasted them. And every new girl who got hired on, they'd warn her about this guy, the guy they called "Mr. Tries Too Hard" behind his back. They'd tell her, "You better try to cum for him 'cause maybe you're the one who can do it and then he'll give up, job well done."

But back then, they didn't know Marcus Handler. They had no idea Mr. Tries Too Hard was destined to become *The Rainmaker*.

I don't know what it was exactly. Maybe it was finding the right girl, or maybe he finally put in his ten thousand hours, you know, the Malcolm Gladwell, key-to-achieving-success-in-anything rule. Maybe it was just blind luck, which makes sense considering he was fingering these girls like a blind kid learning braille. Whatever it was, one of them finally—*sploosh*—she squirted all over the carpet in Room 8, according to the legend. Like her water just broke. Not a single drop of pee, as far as Marcus was concerned.

And look, I'm not here to argue about whether squirting is or isn't piss. We'll leave that to the experts.

But in porn it gets a little hazier, especially in those "squirt bukkake" videos. In them, sure, it's probably *mostly* pee. We get the girls all liquored up with coolers and whatnot, and they're practically ready to burst before it's even their turn for the money shot. Sometimes the bukkakers'll have to double or triple up on the bukkakee because they can't hold it any longer.

But some women, if they sign on as the bukkakee instead of one of the bukkakers, they don't realize they're gonna be pissed on practically non-stop for up to an hour. They don't realize if they get it in the eyes— or *when* they get it in the eyes, I should say, 'cause *they're gonna* get it in the eyes—it's gonna sting. So sometimes you gotta cut a scene short when the first-time bukkakee decides she's had enough after ten or twelve girls mostly pissing in her face. We had one squirt bukkake that ended in a fistfight between the bukkakee and one of the bukkakers. Yanked the weave right off her, gave the poor girl, who was just trying to do her job —and doing it well, I should add—a black eye and busted nose.

It's like they say: it's all fun and games until you get it in the eyes.

And here's a little tidbit of insider information you don't get in those videos: it gets messy. And if the girls ate something they shouldn't have the night before— asparagus, fish, too much garlic—it can *stink* too.

Anyways, that's all to say that in porn, it's mostly pee. But once The Rainmaker made his name, you didn't see a trace of yellow. You couldn't tag these videos "golden shower" or "piss play." The German and Czech markets didn't go wild over them. This was clear or cloudy fluid, splashing out of them. Not trickles. Not streams. *Splashing*.

Oh, you've seen some? Done your research, huh? That's good. Most writers, they do a surface level background check, a few Wiki articles, maybe look me up on Luke Is Back.

The man's a legend, right? Nobody, and I mean *nobody*, has covered porn news and gossip as long as he has. Bill Margold, you know, the director, I think he said it best when he said "Luke Ford is exactly what we (meaning the industry) deserve."

Yeah, I did read what he wrote about me. I'm not saying I agree with everything he's printed, nor what he's said about what happened at the Power Station, but...

You know, nobody's really taken the adult film industry seriously, not since they stopped showing premieres in theatres. You can't get a so-called "real" film critic to review your movie these days no matter how damned artsy or earnest it is. I mean, look at *Caligula* from 1979. Peter O'Toole, Malcolm McDowell, Helen Mirren *and* John Gielgud, with a script by the legendary Gore Vidal, and directed by noted avant-garde filmmaker, Tinto Brass. I'm one hundred percent certain if Bob Guccione didn't go and add all those hardcore sex scenes in it, it could've gotten a Palme D'Or. Same goes for my film *I Am Curious (Red)*. That was a damned good film, if I do say so myself. Well-written, expertly shot, and Tammy Rivers acted the shit outta that role. Not a single nomination, aside from the AVNs.

No, that's not really what I'm looking for when I make films. I don't need respect from Hollywood or awards, if I'm honest. I just feel like porn gets a bad rap, for whatever reason. Making love, now that's beautiful. Making love *on camera*? Disgusting, deplorable, lascivious. *Shameful*, even.

It's a stigma, and it pisses me off. End rant, like they say online.

What were we talking about? Right, Marcus Handler.

Once Marcus found the right girl, word spread pretty quickly among the dancers, and suddenly they were all lining up to see if it really worked or if that one time was just a fluke. But since they remembered how raw he'd made them on his earlier attempts, nobody wanted to take one for the team.

Well, finally Tammy came back to town. She'd been in LA for a while shooting scenes with some very big names, and she'd become something of a minor celebrity around here, especially among the other girls at the Canadian Ballet. And the Ballet itself was getting a lot more popular at the time, seeing as I advertised on all my videos that you could watch these girls dance live and in person for your own personal pleasure, some of them five nights a week.

So Tammy came waltzing back into town and immediately called me up, said, "Let's go see the show," by which she meant Poncho Night, which had just started its long-time engagement at the Ballet.

Of course, I said, "Sure thing." I was busier than I'd even been but I've always got time for the woman who helped make my name. And I was usually at the Ballet or one of the other clubs in town once or twice a week anyway, scouting for new talent, fresh faces.

No, I never did any of the gay clubs, or male strippers. Only shot gay porn once. Why? 'Cause I didn't wanna ruin sex for myself, if I'm honest. I knew if I started down that road I'd just be thinking about work every time I tried to get my rocks off. Like, how his legs would look better with his knees positioned a little higher up, or could he look back at me just so as he's getting fucked, and is the lighting just right in this room or do I need another fill on the far wall? Stuff like that.

Anyway, they always say not to mix business with pleasure, and I definitely did not wanna be the kind of guy who gets high on his own supply, if that makes sense.

So Tammy and me, we go to the Ballet that night with our ponchos, and after the splash show, Tammy hears from one or two of the dancers there's this guy they call Mr. Tries Too Hard, only it seemed like he tried so hard he finally actually *did*. They tell her this one girl, who wasn't on shift that night, just "gushed absolute buckets," their words, from barely five minutes of fingerbanging, and they wanna know if it's true, if he's finally discovered the secret to making *any woman squirt* like he'd always been promising. But nobody wants to risk getting their insides pounded like a pork tenderloin again.

Tammy being Tammy, she was up for anything, so she says, "Point him out."

Marcus wasn't there yet, but he always showed up on a Wednesday night, and true to form, he strode in like the cock of the walk about an hour later. Tammy being Tammy walks right up to him at his regular table where he's nursing his first of two Coors Lights, and says, "I hear you're some kind of pussy tamer. Think you're man enough to tame *this* kitty?"

Of course, Marcus knew exactly who she was, everyone at the Ballet did back then, and he was hot to try his supposedly magic fingers on her. So Tammy suggests the three of us skip on over to the Lonely Motel in her brand-new Cobra Mustang to test out his skills.

We weren't there but three minutes and Marcus is already taking off his clothes. I say, "It's not that kind of shoot, Marcus."

"Yeah," Tammy says. "We didn't come here to fuck. In all my years getting fucked on camera, I've never once found anyone who can make me squirt. If you can do that, honey, Chucky here can make you a star."

I didn't want to make any promises, but of course I brought my camera—which was one of the top prosumer models at the time, a Panasonic HC-X2100—so I said, "Sure thing," and we started shooting.

Now it turned out Marcus couldn't get women to squirt from any position, not the way he'd figured out through trial and error during his seven- or eight-year porn career. Tammy had to lie face-down on the bed with her ass in the air and her legs off the edge, which wasn't great for a single-camera shoot, since I had to go back and forth around the end of the bed to get her reaction shots, and closeups on her pussy while Marcus plied his trade. Meaning, when the grand finale finally happened I'd just better hope I was on the right end of her at the time, or I'd miss most of the water works.

That, plus when Marcus got down on his knees and made a gesture like Spider-Man shooting web, then slipped the middle two fingers into her pussy—which she'd shaved into a neat little landing strip as was the style at the time, before everyone decided hairless was cleaner or made them look younger or some shit, and they all started doing full Brazilian—you could barely see any of her genitals with Marcus's pinky and index fingers sticking out on either side.

It wasn't exactly my best work, is what I'm saying. But got a ton of hits and downloads, 'cause it was another First Time Video, it being the first time Tammy Rivers actually lived up to her name.

It wasn't exactly magic, not like that first girl claimed it was, but he did something with his fingers, just pulling up up up like he was pull-starting a motorboat at ten-times speed, and it started to sound like he was stirring a yogurt pot inside her cooch. Then all of a sudden, Tammy starts moaning, only her body's shaking from his fingering so her moan is like, "*Oh-oh-oh-oh-oh!*" Like those videos Howard Stern used to do with women riding those Sybian saddles.

Then *sploosh*—this absolute geyser starts spraying out her, and Marcus immediately pulls out his fingers and starts rubbing her clit side to side, making her fluids spray all over the place. The bed, the floor, my camera, all the way up to the fucking ceiling. And meanwhile, The Rainmaker's down there on all fours—well, three technically, 'cause the fourth's still doing its magic—he's kneeling there, right in the splashzone, lapping at her pussy like a dog getting a drink from a water fountain.

I'd done a lot of squirt stuff by then—like I said, some of it was piss play—but this was *something else*. He must've gotten her squirting like ten times in the span of five minutes. In the end it truly was magical. Like a shaman bringing the rain after a year-long drought. Hence the name we gave.

That's what I said when Tammy couldn't take anymore and collapsed on the bed, exhausted. I said "He's like a rainmaker," and Tammy sighed real heavily and says, "That's what we should call him," 'cause in that moment she decided she wanted to come back and work with me. Not *for* me. *With* me.

Marcus, lying on the soggy carpet in his drenched suit, he raised his head like a sleeping dog and looks at both of us, me sitting in the cuck chair drying off my camera with a hand towel from the bathroom, hoping like hell it wasn't broken, Tammy with her head hanging over the edge of the bed in a blissful haze.

Marcus asks us, "Did I do good?"

"You did *really* fucking good," Tammy answered for me, and I said, "Dude, if this doesn't make you a star, I don't know what will."

Sure enough, I posted the video that same night and within two days it was our most-viewed in over a year. The Rainmaker was true to his name, he really did save us from drought. Not that we were in danger of going bankrupt or anything, at least not that year, but after Tammy left to become the star she was destined to be, none of our videos went viral until the now-legendary *Tammy Rivers Meets The Rainmaker*.

After that, all the girls on the Powerplay roster, my Angels, wanted to take their turn riding Marcus Handler. And it turned out despite all his overcompensating to make women squirt, The Rainmaker had a pretty decent-sized tool, and he got pretty good at fucking with a little direction from yours truly.

What I said before, about Tammy wanting to work with me? She decided she wanted to put some of the money she'd been saving into Powerplay, so I made her a partner. Most people don't know that 'cause she was a silent partner for a long while, but she's the one who put the downpayment on the warehouse.

It was a dump when we found it, used to be a Spirit Halloween with a ton of fire and water damage, but the price was definitely right. We weren't gonna put the Armory building in San Francisco to shame or anything. You know, the one Kink.com owned for little over a decade? But they didn't move operations there until 2006, so while just about everyone else was still shooting out of a van or moving from one motel room or rented luxury home to the next, we were the only porn site that I know of to have our own massive studio aside from Kink.

That's not to say we stopped shooting videos at the Lonely Motel. Most of the so-called "amateur" stuff we shot for a while was here, for that authentic amateur feel. We also replicated one of the rooms at the Power Station, complete with a working exterior wall and door, so folks who wanted to get that true Powerplay feel in their videos could shoot their own amateur stuff without having to worry about how many people came on the sheets before them.

Not this room, no. Room 6, actually. It has a... *strange* history, let's say. A lot of crazy things happened in that room, but that's where I started my interviews with the dancers from the Canadian Ballet, and where Tammy fucked that bottle of Miller High Life. Actually, it's where I shot the majority of our early stuff. I just got used to the room, and whenever it was free, that's the one I'd rent. So I wanted to pay homage, I guess, to the room where I got my start.

But... we were talking about The Rainmaker. You got me jumping ahead again. Let's get back on track, huh?

So after that first video went viral, all the girls wanted a ride on The Rainmaker. We started shooting squirt bukkake videos in the warehouse. This was before we even had a name for the place. We just called it "the warehouse."

The Rainmaker, he'd sit in the middle of a crowd of naked women on our first makeshift bedroom set—a reverse gangbang, they call it in the industry—he'd get each one of them started with his Spider-Man web-slinger technique, then he'd drop down and just get absolutely *drenched* in their cum. Drinking it, gargling it, spitting it back into their mouths. You name it. It was gross, it was glorious, but most of all: it was a *goldmine*.

We ran into all kinds of problems shooting this stuff, though. Slippery floors, sprained ankles, broken cameras. You name it. But it was all in the name of making art, so it was all good.

And Marcus Handler, he became a hero to millions of young men who wanted nothing more than to please as many women as possible, and in those early days of "game theory"—you know, the whole thing about a unified, applied theory for seducing women, signaling, negging and all that, like the guy Tom Cruise played in *Magnolia*, "respect the cock, tame the cunt"—all of this was tapping directly into the cultural zeitgeist.

This was over a decade before "toxic masculinity" and all that. Experts in this field used to be called "players," or "pickup artists." I guess they just call them "fuckbois" now.

Right, "fuckboi" with an I not a Y.

But most of the men who looked up to him, who wanted to *be* him, they were just normal guys tired of not being able to get laid. Tired of being seen as the "nice guy," always put in the "friend zone." I mean, anyone can understand that, right? We've all been in that position once or twice, even me. I've had a few droughts here and there. Not many, but a few. I've put men on a pedestal and ruined any chance of a relationship. I've wanted more from guys who just wanted to be friends. Haven't you?

See? Gay, straight, lesbian, bi—it's the one universal constant. And sure, maybe their response to it isn't entirely *moral*. But dating *is* a game. If there's a cheat code, who wouldn't try to use it?

Anyway, all that is to say that Marcus Handler aka The Rainmaker became an overnight phenomenon. And the fact that he actually *respected* the women he was fucking was just the icing on the cake. He was the polar opposite of all those so-called fuckbois and players. He respected a woman's limits and always asked for consent. In an industry where the lines can sometimes blur, that's refreshing, though I'd never hire an Angel who *didn't* respect consent. And yes, we consider all cis and trans male, female and nonbinary stars "Angels."

Charlie's Angels, that's right. We just thought it would be fun, even though I prefer Chuck.

What I'm saying is, Marcus wasn't the Andrew Tate of porn or anything like that. He was a goddamn paragon in the industry, a true gentleman, and a close personal friend. It just so happened he was addicted to getting women off, which I'm sure you'll agree, when it comes to addictions, it isn't all that bad.

I assume you heard about his tragic death. The last film we did together, we called it *The Rainmaker Does Gitmo*. In retrospect it was a poor choice of title, and an absolutely reckless idea. But one morning over coffee at the Land's End Diner, which you probably passed on your drive here, Marcus came to me with an idea: he wanted to do a video where he's a prisoner at Guantanamo Bay and all the women are guards. Uniforms, nightsticks, handcuffs, the whole shebangs. They handcuff him in this prison cell we made in the warehouse, which was actually more like a real jail cell than the all-white rooms they had at Gitmo. Then they take turns fucking him, fucking each other with the nightsticks, sucking them, sucking him, scissoring, all that fun stuff.

The thing he told me was, to him, or the role he's playing, it's all cruel and unusual punishment. This shit is against the Geneva Conventions. The Rainmaker is a prisoner and he is most definitely *not* consenting.

This was in that hot minute when CNC, or Consensual Non-Consensual porn, was all the rage. I didn't want anything to do with that stuff, and I made that clear on my site. No fantasy rape shit. No revenge porn. No kidnapping and forced into fucking. No coercion. No sleep fucking. None of that.

I reiterated that to Marcus, and he says, "You're living in the past, Chucky-baby. Besides, this is *reverse* rape fantasy. I promise you, this is every man's dream."

"Not mine," I said.

"Every *straight* guy's," he says.

And I don't know. I guess I can't speak to that. Would I want to be ravaged by a pack of horny men? No. I'm a one-man guy. I had one or two threesomes in my single year of college, but I learned pretty quick it wasn't for me.

Do I judge people who fantasize about being raped? Cummed on by multiple partners? Toe-fucking? Hell no. Not only because kink is my bread and butter, but I strongly believe no one should have any say in what other people find sexy, what turns them on, so long as it's not against the law or harming anyone else without their consent.

That's my philosophy. You can write that down.

I know you're recording this, but seriously. Underline that shit in your article. *Twice.*

No one should have any say in what turns other people on, so long as it's not against the law or harming people without their consent.

All right, I'll get off my high horse now.

Where were we?

Right, *The Rainmaker Does Gitmo.*

Fuck.

What a clusterfuck that was. I should've listened to the signs. And the universe or whatever was giving me plenty of signs. Like when I woke up and that song came on when I flicked on MTV. You know that song: "Isn't it ironic?"

Yeah, the one that's just a bunch of minor inconveniences. But I figure it probably wouldn't have had the same impact if she sang "Isn't it coincidental?" Don't you think?

Then I found out Marcus's lead costar, Virginia Adams, is a fucking *Scorpio.* Marcus was an Aquarius, and the two generally don't pair well together. Like fire and gasoline. Not to mention Mercury was in retrograde at the time, which made it worse.

All that's to say, I should've seen the signs. Especially since I was reluctant to shoot the damn thing in the first place. I should've listened to my gut and told Marcus thanks but no thanks. But I didn't. I admit, I was thinking about chasing trends. And Marcus was right, the trend was shifting toward CNC, despite how I felt about the whole subgenre.

So we shot it.

It even started out bad. Virginia got a little too much into her role as the warden—I don't even know if Gitmo *had* wardens, if I'm honest, but ninety-nine percent of our viewers probably didn't either. She nearly broke Marcus's nose shoving him up against those bars. It was so bad we had to take five so he could ice his face or he'd end up shooting the rest of it with a black eye. No coverup in the world could withstand that much gushing to the face.

But after that, we got into the groove of it. Marcus had his usual Diet Coke while the ladies had coolers and whatnot. That was just to loosen them up, not to fill their bladders. This wasn't a champagne shower. Marcus always brought his A-game when it came to his *nom de porn*, and his final performance was no exception.

So anyway, one of the girls got the bright idea they should *waterboard* him with their cum. I didn't want to participate in that. I was adamantly against it. But Marcus, who was normally one hundred percent committed to consent... I don't want to speak ill of the dead, but he coerced me into it.

"Don't be a *pussy*, Chucky-baby," he kept saying. "This is avant-garde shit, man. This is *Gonzo*. One day people will look back on this video and say, 'This is it. This is the one video that *changed the game*.'" And all the girls agreed, it really would stand out. I figure they all had their eyes on that same AVN award Tammy just got. You know, Most Outrageous Sex Scene.

Look, I'm not shirking responsibility. I agreed to it. I filmed it. But if he'd spent more time pressing their fuck buttons and less time pressing me to do the waterboarding, and if the girls hadn't *agreed* with him, and if Marcus hadn't been such a close personal friend of mine, I never would've said yes.

In retrospect, obviously, I should've listened to my gut. But Marcus was right, *The Rainmaker Does Gitmo* really did change the game. Isn't that ironic? That single movie is why you never saw anyone in the industry do squirt waterboarding ever again.

Go figure.

So how it worked was, they laid the towel over Marcus's face, and the five of them squatted over him with Virginia riding his cock and holding his arms down, while the six of them—Virginia included, she could squirt from penetration—they just absolutely *showered* him in cum. Probably some piss too, if I'm honest. And Marcus, he did his job, acting like he was mortally against it. Like they were doing him grievous harm. Only, like I said, it turned out they were, consensual or not.

He drowned, yeah. Technically it was a *near*-drowning. He drowned but we *revived* him. Virginia was a lifeguard in high school, knew exactly what to do when he stopped breathing. Mouth to mouth. Pumping his chest. All of that.

And he came back. He coughed up a lungful of pussy juice, everyone sighed and applauded, and he really did seem fine after that. Did his post-video interview, laughing and chatting with the ladies, drinking Diet Coke while they had beers and coolers.

But triumph is always a heartbeat away from tragedy, that's something I've learned over the years, as an artist. The only thing that comes easy is a first-time male performer, and if something seems too easy, well...

Everything comes with a price, right? You pay it now, or you pay it later. Call it karma. Call it fate.

I call it *life*.

For Marcus, his trouble started that night. He goes home, starts coughing real bad. Calls in sick the next day. I mean, this is a guy who would go out of his way to come in for a shoot. He was doing the work he was put on this earth to do, there was never any doubt about that. The man *never* took PTO. But he called in sick. I should've put two and two together right then, told him to go to the emergency room, but I didn't. I was too busy editing the video to get it up on the site.

Next day, TMZ says he's dead. His girlfriend found him in his condo bringing him his morning Mean Green Juice. By then the video was already doing great. Traffic got so high the site crashed. So we had to do a lot of damage control before we were even able to decide whether or not we were gonna pull the video.

In the end, we decided to keep it up. It was a six in one, half dozen in the other situation. Yes, it was terrible he died, and it seemed to some people—those ghoulish celebrity bloggers, for instance—like maybe we were capitalizing off his death. But we didn't know how he died. We didn't know liquid could've stayed in his lungs, and he could still die from it even after he'd been brought back from the brink.

And anyway, the way we figured, Marcus would've *wanted* us to keep it on the site. The man died doing what he loved. How many of us can really say that?

Sometimes bad things happen, right? Sometimes you get a gut feeling, but you don't trust your gut and it happens anyway, and you think, "We could've avoided all this if I'd listened to my gut."

Sometimes I think—and I'm not the only one— sometimes I wonder if starting our careers here, at the Lonely Motel, if it didn't put a curse on us. It got us to the top, sure, but only because the higher you are, the harder you fall.

Sometimes I think that, anyway.

Sometimes I think it's all a load of crap.

Because *that's life*. Bad things happen all the time, to good people and bad people. And when it happens, you have to pivot. You have to pick up the pieces and move on, and hopefully to greener pastures.

When the autopsy results came back saying Marcus died of pulmonary edema, also known as "dry drowning," of course we decided to pull the video. But by then, all the fucking tube sites—Pornhub, xHamster, all those scumfucks—they'd already spread it all over the net. We filed DMCA complaints, but you can never really get those things entirely scrubbed.

Right, unless you're a senator. He went scorched earth. Took Google to court over it too, not just us.

The day of Marcus's funeral—I haven't seen that many porn people outside of the AVNs. The man truly was a legend, and everyone who worked with him only had nice things to say. The eulogies lasted two hours. That's longer than most of them can last in bed, and trust me, we have to edit a lot down for time.

Marcus Handler, aka The Rainmaker, he was a consummate performer. He was a class act, and despite what I might think about what happened that day on set, I'm still proud to call him my friend.

Rest in peace, Marcus.

No, I'm fine, thank you. I appreciate it.

What's next? Well, before we get to all that other stuff, I guess I better tell you about—

THE POWER STATION

We called it that for obvious reasons, my last name—Power—being one, but also because it was in a run-down neighborhood literally right across the street from one of those hydroelectric substations with all the towers. That's why we used those towers as part of our production logo, with the little lightning effects. Sort of reminiscent of the old RKO Pictures vanity card, with the radio transmitter on top of the spinning globe. Right, the one before all the old Orson Welles flicks.

So after Tammy and I bought the Power Station, I was eager to expand, and we hired on more staff. College kids, mostly. Film and TV students from my alma mater, Buffalo State, and also from UB. Some local, some not. We gave these kids a crash course in film-making their university education never would've prepared them for. Tarantino famously said, "When people ask if I went to film school, I say, 'No, I went to *films*.'" That's my experience, despite the single year I dropped out of.

What's that?

Where'd you get my *transcript* from?

She did? That catty bitch. I love her to death, but that was a low blow, even for her.

Fine. I *failed* out of film school. But I wasn't really interested in theory and critique and all that crap. I already learned all that stuff studying movies and screenplays and reading books on film on my own time during high school. I wanted to *make films*. And I *was* making them. Just not for class.

That's true, I did almost get kicked out mid-semester for making a porn film with the school equipment. I wanted to do this faux-vintage thing, got some kids from the drama program to help with costumes, hair and makeup. I wanted to make the filthiest vintage stag reel anyone'd ever seen. Those French loops from the '20s are pretty rare, so I wanted to make one that would cause a stir among collectors. I called it *A Champagne Shower for Collette*. So it would be the oldest watersports film ever discovered, if we'd been able to upload it anonymously to the internet.

Stag reels?

They're sort of proto-porn. Porn films before *films* were really even a thing. Porn did everything first. *Everything*. Before Georges Méliès crashed a lunar lander into the eye of the moon. Before the Lumière Brothers terrified theater-goers with a train pulling into La Ciotat Station. Porn was there first, captivating audiences with candid reels of stripteases and fucking.

Long story short, as this is yet another tangent, we used their vintage 16mm camera, a Ciné-Kodak, and the dean got pissed when she found out I used up all the old reels they had shooting the damn thing. She threatened to expel me and everyone involved in making the movie if I didn't destroy the film, even the poor kids doing the damn makeup.

I wasn't even able to transfer the footage to digital before someone squealed, and if I had... I don't know what I would've done. Maybe kept it for myself, you know, for posterity. Maybe released it out of spite. Anyway, I cut up the film while she watched me do it. I guess I could've pulled the old switcheroo if I'd been clever enough. Get another old can of 16-mill and cut that up instead.

Needless to say, I didn't do that, and nobody got expelled. I failed out in the second semester, but by then Tammy's FTV had already exploded, so I didn't really give two shits. I didn't need a diploma or a doctorate. I wasn't planning to *teach*. I wanted to *make* art, not *talk about it*.

So like I was saying, nothing can prepare you for the real world like hands-on experience. And as good as some of these programs might be, they'll never be as beneficial to starting your career as real-world experience will be.

You got your MFA, I bet. And what do you do with it now? Paperweight? Collecting dust in some box in the closet under a bunch of shoes?

See what I mean? I bet they didn't even care about your degree when they hired you, did they? Probably read your prior work and based it on that. Oh, you're freelance? A *hired gun*. I love that. It sounds sexy when you call it that.

Hired gun.

Anyway, we had kids from the local colleges on our crews. All of legal age, of course. And they weren't doing anything *in front* of the camera, let's be clear. This was a serious place of business and we meant to keep it that way.

How?

Well, for instance, there was an incident with one of the kids. Turned out he only wanted to work with us so he could get close to one of my Angels.

I'd rather not say her name. You know, for her privacy.

So this kid, he ended up becoming our go-to boom mic operator. The kid looked like a weakling but he could stand there holding the boom above his head for hours without even the slightest quiver. And that's a tough job. People flame out quick because it's physically exhausting. You ever try to get a spider web down from a high corner with a broom? Or put a new bulb in a ceiling light? Try holding that position for hours on end.

Now this kid, he's right there on set while this woman, the object of his affection, did her thing. After a while, she realizes he's staring at her the whole shoot, tent in his shorts. So she tells me. Not to get him in trouble, just that she thought it was cute and funny. He's got a little crush. She's in her thirties, meaning she's already doing MILF porn at this time, but also, she's been around long enough to've practically seen it all.

No, it wasn't any of those guys. And I told you, that subject is off-limits. Please respect that.

So after a while she starts noticing this kid is watching her while she's leaving the Power Station, from his car. No lights on. Just sitting there in the dark of the parking lot. The next day she comes to me, saying she's pretty sure this kid followed her home. Kid comes in to work, says how ya doin, gets a coffee, same old routine. Then he turns to her with a big goofy smile and says "How was your night, so-and-so?"

She snaps. She starts screaming like a banshee and

runs at him. Starts throttling him right there in front of everyone.

We broke it up. He's got bruises around his neck, she's broken a fingernail, but no serious injuries. So I had to make a tough decision, right there. Do I let my go-to boom mic operator go because of a suspicion, or do I fire one of my longest-running Angels for trying to murder him in front of the cast and crew?

I fired her. What else could I do? If I let her off the hook for trying to choke someone to death in my place of business, how would that look? What kind of precedent would that set?

The kid? Yeah, he ended up doing the same thing to a new Angel a couple of months later. So I made the wrong call. I should've fired *both* their asses. But without evidence, it was the only call I could make. Don't worry, I threw his creeper ass out the door when it happened again. Made sure he was blackballed from the industry too.

Her? She was fine. She worked with all the big names after that, Vivid, Bangbros, MYLF, you name it. She wasn't gonna let one little pervert bring her down, and nobody on set that day would've said a word about why I let her go. They all loved her, and with good reason. I mean, there were rumors about an altercation, yeah. But I never confirmed anything. Just said she was always very professional to work with but we had "creative differences."

She never held it against me, no. In fact, she came back to work with me again a year or so later. Water under the bridge.

But that's what I mean about serious, about professional. The Power Station is a place of business, and after that incident we hired someone to handle HR issues. You've got a beef with me or a coworker, you took it up with Nancy in HR.

Like what?

Okay, this is a weird one but it's relevant.

One day we were doing a fisting scene. Girl-on-girl. Vaginal fisting, anal fisting, prolapsed assholes gaping like goldfish lips, the whole shebangs. Yeah, I'm not a big fan either, but it sells, and I'm not gonna kinkshame or complain when it pays the bills.

It's a three girl scene and these girls are going at it. In up to their wrists, two of them just churning butter in this Angel's pussy and asshole simultaneously, in, out, in, out. Then all of a sudden, I get a whiff of this smell. Like... like rotting cabbage, or like one of our toilets backed up.

The crew start plugging their noses. Wafting their hands in front of their faces. The boom mic kid, the one I told you about, he lets the pole fall for probably the first time in his career. His face is literally *green*.

Then one of the girls throws up. The other girl sees her puke and pukes herself, all over the prolapsed asshole she's up to her wrist in. The two of them yank their fists out with this double-pop sound like two champagne corks popped at once, and the stink *intensifies*. It's like standing over an open sewer.

The girl, she's covered in two different brands of puke, and then *she* pukes. Then the boom mic kid throws up a gutful of black coffee and crullers. My PA, she can't hold it in any longer and *she* chucks up the spaghetti she had the night before.

You know that scene from *Stand By Me*, with the fat kid making everyone puke? It was like that but in real life. Even the reek of eight people's vomit couldn't overpower the putrid stench of that woman's untreated gonorrhea.

So I call "cut," and we all run for the washrooms. Candy Rains is already standing at the slop sink we use for when we're painting the sets, scrubbing her hands with turpentine like Lady Macbeth washing away the blood. "Out, damned spot!" Only she's probably thinking, "Out, damned stench!"

Meanwhile the offender, the woman with the untreated STI, she scurries off set, vomit dripping off her naked body on her way to the showers.

After we all get cleaned up and Ms. Smelly Cat's applied her ointment or whatever—the smell is thankfully gone, whatever it was she did to it—I'm sitting there in Nancy the HR Lady's office with these three women, trying to come up with some sort of response to what happened.

All I could say is, "Look, I'm sure we can all agree this got way out of hand."

And the whole room went silent for a few seconds. Then Nancy and Ms. Smelly Cat and her costars all crack up. I didn't even mean it as a joke so I'm sitting there staring with a stupid look on my face for a second, trying to figure out why everyone's laughing. Then I get it, and I'm laughing too.

So anyway, after we all had a good laugh, Ms. Smelly Cat admits she forgot to use her ointment the past two days and she didn't think gonorrhea was transmittable from hand to vaginal contact, so she didn't tell anyone. She apologized, the Angels all shook hands—freshly scrubbed—and we called it a day.

Hand on heart, that's the absolute truth.

But that's the Power Station. We may have our political differences, we may not agree on every little thing, but when shit hits the fan—or vaginal discharge, in this case—we *hash it out*. Nancy tried her best to be impartial, and she was nearly always right. She wasn't friends with any of us outside of work either. She'd been working in the finance sector for thirty years before we found her at a temp agency, because other companies thought she was too old to hire on full-time.

For the most part it was like a great big family. We all broke bread together, drank together, smoked weed together, went to the same parties, shared each other's successes and failures. I can honestly say without any hyperbole, that was one of the best periods of my life.

And yes, we did release that video. I don't generally like to put my name on that kind of filth, but it did get us nominated for Most Outrageous Sex Scene that year.

Speaking of outrageous sex scenes, I should tell you about this one video we did, and it also ties in to the whole "curse" thing. Can we keep this one off the record though? Is that possible?

Great.

So this is one of only a handful of times I strayed from the path of ethical pornographer into Gonzo filmmaker territory. You know, the sort of shit Filthy Lessons and BangBus were into, before the Filthy Lessons crew got murdered by a girl claiming she was "possessed" by the ghost of one of their earlier performers, of all things, and before BangBus got bought by the Czech company who also owns *Penthouse* and a couple of the tube sites.

So one day an old friend of mine I hadn't seen in ages comes to me with something he wants to do. He was off in LA for a while becoming a pretty successful sushi chef apparently, but he came back home for reasons that aren't particularly pertinent to this story. One day we're talking and he comes at me with a proposal for a revenge porn, which under normal circumstances I'd be adamantly against, like I said. But this wasn't your regular get-back-at-your-ex-by-leaking-your-home-sex-tapes thing. His idea was a blackmail tape to get back at the guy who fucked up his whole life and was trying to extort money out of him. And since me and this guy, let's call him Johnny, went all the way back to high school, I said "Why not?"

The other guy, he was what they used to call a "wankster" back in the day. He called himself "Juicy," if that gives you any indication of the kind of dude he was. This is a real bad dude. A heroin dealer. A murderer by proxy. An extortionist. Scumfuck extraordinaire, in other words. Plus, he had a tendency to say things like "know'm sayin" and drop N-bombs like it was a Tourette's vocal tic, which annoyed the shit outta me and frankly would've disgusted me even if my husband —who was still my boyfriend at the time—wasn't a black man.

So I don't feel bad at all for what we did that day, which was pretty much just a fun little prank video featuring anal sex and a lot of fake blood, costarring one of my former Angels, Candy Rains, the dancer who does Poncho Night at the Ballet. I won't bore you with the details of the shoot, the asscheek motorboating and all of that, but by the end of it, this guy Juicy was running out of the room with his pants around his ankles, screaming like a... well, like Juicy himself probably would've called a "little bitch."

Anyway the next time Juicy comes to threaten Johnny about the money he claims he's owed, Johnny pops in the DVD with an instant replay of Juicy fleeing from what he probably thought was a murder scene, screaming like a little bitch. Johnny tells him if he doesn't leave him alone, that this is just a copy, and I'm just waiting on his word to post it all over the internet.

Juicy's worried about the cops. He still thinks he might've killed Candy Rains. But also, he's worried about looking like a "pussy." So he gives up leaning on Johnny for the money and I guess he must've paid it back to his employers out of his own pocket, or the debt never existed in the first place. But rumors spread about the video anyway, as they do, and eventually his employers caught wind of it and fired his candy ass.

The rest of his life was just as awful, from what I heard, and before we get back to talking about the Power Station, this'll probably interest you, since some people seem to believe it ties in to the so-called "Chuck P. Curse."

After Juicy lost his very reputable job dealing heroin, he apparently got into luring in young women, mostly immigrants and indigenous women, for this big-time trafficking ring who were running girls in and out of Canada. I guess he was working alongside this other scumfuck, some "Romeo pimp," they call them, but I don't know all the details for certain. This is mostly just what I heard, like I said. I don't know how much of it is true, but I know for sure how it ended.

Anyway, *I heard* Juicy and this pimp were using the Lonely Motel as a sort of temporary holding location for these women, before they loaded them up into the backs of transport trucks with no air-conditioning and very little water, to run them across the border.

The shit they put these women through is absolutely horrifying, which is why I didn't shed a single tear when I heard the cops found Juicy dead in one of the rooms here. *Apparently* a woman he'd been "seasoning," as these scumfucks so elegantly call it, she hit her breaking point after too much psychological and physical abuse and managed to get loose while Juicy was out getting take-out at a nearby gas station. He comes back to the room and *bam*—she slams into him, cuts his throat from ear to ear with a bottle cap, then runs screaming into the night, sort of like Juicy did the day we shot that video with him and Candy Rains. Only this poor girl *really did* leave a dead body behind, lying in a puddle of blood and fruit punch.

The girl? She was never caught, no. And I can't say I blame her for what she did, not that I condone murder. The world is better off without him in it. And she's certainly better off now, wherever she is.

This whole *curse* thing, though? I think that's always been less about me than about *this place*, even though a lot of it could be tied to me *tangentially*. Like I said, the Lonely Motel leaves a mark on you. It takes its toll. Marcus paid it. So did Juicy. So did our erstwhile boom mic operator, who was shot outside a woman's home when she caught him peeping through her bathroom window.

And we were about to pay some of that toll ourselves.

Around that time, the tube sites started running rampant with pirated videos, all the little fish porn companies got swallowed up by the big fish, and industry revenue dropped all across the boards. Then the financial crisis hit us even harder in 2008.

We were struggling, if I'm honest. And the bigger fish had their eyes on swallowing us up along with all the other little indie sites. This was before MindGeek practically took over the entire industry. BangBros, Brazzers, Digital Playground, Vivid, Wicked—you name it, we got offers from all of them. But I flat-out refused to sell, no matter how much anyone offered us.

I've always said my purpose in life is to provide pleasure for other people. That's my kink, let's say. And Tammy, as my then-silent partner, she agreed.

She was still flying back and forth from LA at the time—this was before she moved back to Buffalo to help take care of day-to-day operations—and she was able to round up enough investors from La La Land to keep us afloat until I could figure out where to take Powerplay next.

And where to take it, I decided after some long, difficult introspection, was to file Chapter 11, take out a second mortgage on the Power Station, and use the income we had left to start—

BESPOKE.COM

So my original idea with Bespoke was to give people exactly the experience they want in their porn. You wanna watch a couple of furries in wolf costumes rubbing up against each other until they cum, what they call yiffing? You got it. You wanna see a chick slather herself in ketchup and mustard and some dude in a hot dog costume eat it off her naked body? Here you go.

Basically I wanted to make Bespoke "the Burger King of Porn." *Have it your way*, you know? And Tammy thought the idea was brilliant.

Those are real examples of custom videos we've made, by the way. And that's not to kinkshame or anything. I'm just telling you, we've had some... let's say *interesting* requests.

That thing they say about the internet, Rule 34: *If it exists, there's a porn of it*? I don't know if that was true *before* Bespoke, but it's certainly truer since we got in the game, and even more so since other producers joined us.

The thing is, a lot of it isn't even *porn* at all, not technically. We've done everything from positive affirmation videos to wet and messy or tickle fetish. Yes, the vast majority is still sexually explicit content. Even so, most of it is more like... *wish fulfilment*. Like psychodramas in therapy. Or role-play.

An example?

Okay. Well, there was this one individual who wanted us to shoot a video with the performer play-acting as his mother, telling him he's loved, that he was never an accident, that her and his dad gave him up because they were too young, too financially unstable, and were never meant for each other.

Doesn't that just break your heart?

Did it work?

Well, probably not, if I'm honest, all things considered. But that's beside the point, isn't it? These videos aren't meant to cure people of all their psychological maladies. They aren't *magic bullets*. When you take an aspirin, do you expect it to prevent any and all potential headaches you might have in the future, or just to soothe the one you're suffering from *in that moment*?

Right. So that's what Bespoke is for our patrons. An *aspirin for the soul*, let's say. A soothing balm.

Or maybe you just wanna jerk off to a clown riding a tricycle and rubbing her tits with balloons once in a while. Who am I to judge?

So our purpose, our *raison d'être*, has always been to "make fantasies come true" for our patrons, like our slogan said on the site. Be it a guy who wants a bunch of naked women to tear up all the clothes his ex-wife left in their house when she abandoned him for another man in the middle of the night, to a woman who just wants to watch a man beat off with a traffic cone stuck halfway up his ass.

Sure, of course it's also to make money. Gotta keep the lights on, right? And with Bespoke, we brought in anywhere from five hundred bucks to upwards of thirty, fifty thousand *per video*, depending on the complexity of the request and the costs involved in producing it. There was even that one—the rebirth video that got leaked and went viral—that one cost its patrons two hundred thousand dollars. Now that was for a very *specific* type of client, and I can't even be sure they were getting off on it. Some of these rich guys, they'll pay to watch all kinds of out-there shit just 'cause they can. And anyway, I'm pretty sure there's no laws against what we did there. If there was, I would've gotten arrested for it, wouldn't I?

No, it didn't cost anything to make, aside from the lube. And half of it went to the performers in the video, the other half to cover costs at the Power Station.

That's right. Just like with Powerplay and our Angels, *we're a family*. We take care of our own. We produce ethical pornography, featuring all body types, and we make sure every one of them is paid well over a living wage for their work.

Because, and I'll say it louder for the people in the back, *sex work is real work*.

Exactly. You have to respect the hustle.

Actually, Nancy passed away a few years ago unfortunately. But she stayed with us right until the end. Died with her boots on, as they say. Although she typically wore comfortable shoes.

So we've done it all at Bespoke.com. Giantess videos, diaper fetish, plushophilia—that's a sexual attraction to stuffed toys, which is usually just a lot of rubbing and kissing, but sometimes involves dildos or pocket vaginas fitted into teddy bears and whatnot to fuck. I figure we've done videos for just about every fetish you can imagine, and probably a hundred others you couldn't.

We did this one series of videos, we called it *Karaokkake*. You know, a—what do you call it? Right, a portmanteau, of *karaoke* and *bukkake*. It's exactly what you think it is. We lined up our best singers—ladies, of course—and had them competing in a singing competition, voted on by the viewers just like *American Idol*. Only we had no judge's panel, and these girls were taking wads of cum on their faces while they performed, and the kick was they had to keep on singing like nothing was wrong. Imagine trying to hit the high notes in "I Will Always Love You" while some guy's shooting his baby gravy in your eyes.

The girls loved it. I mean, it was loads of fun, to watch at home and to be a part of shooting. So to speak.

We even did—I think you'll find this is really interesting—we did a handful of videos for a psych evaluation at CNYPC, the mental hospital, with a female performer dry-humping a male mannequin in various ways. This was something I very much didn't wanna get involved in at first, after what the patient did to my friend. But the doctor understood my reservations and assured me the videos wouldn't be used for getting off, they were strictly for therapeutic purposes. Actually, the patient herself told me a couple of years later that after the years she spent held there, and the videos we made for her, she's been entirely cured of her particular ailment. She's moved on, married a nice man, and never once felt the urge to power sander his genitals to a smooth bump like she did to my friend.

I don't like to use that term, but yes, the so-called Mannequin Man is a close personal friend of mine.

No, I'm absolutely certain he *wouldn't* want to participate in an interview, and I flat-out refuse to ask. He couldn't even do it if he wanted to, so let's just move on, okay?

Where the hell was I?

Right, our mission statement. I can say with hand on heart that we did a great job for all of our patrons, or at least as good a job as we were able to at the time. We helped a lot of people, if not psychologically, at least to get their rocks off. And how could anyone look at that as a bad thing?

We've never harmed anybody, at least not intentionally, and everyone we've worked with has been old enough to make their own decisions. We do background checks, but yes, we have and still do hire justice-involved individuals. Be kind of hard not to in a business so heavily criminalized. But we believe strongly in rehabilitation. That's what the criminal justice system is supposed to be for, right? Not just punishment?

I don't know, I'm no therapist. I'm not qualified to speak on the mental well-being of every one of my employees and performers. We didn't do psych evals. This isn't the police academy. Let's just say they all *seemed* sane to me. We do hire a fair amount of folks who consider themselves neurodivergent, or "neurospicy," as one likes to call themself. But no one we'd have considered *dangerous*.

All that is to say our performers are all consenting adults, and any request that crosses a line for them, we veto it. And there've been plenty of vetoes, believe me.

Well, like, there's always someone who sees sploshing, wet and messy fetish—you know, squishing food and the like on your body, your face, between your toes, in your ass crack, your armpits, your pussy—there's always someone who requests chocolate pie or cake or ice cream coming out of someone's asshole. Ever since that goddamn *Two Girls One Cup* video, someone always wants "chocolate (something) coming out of their ass," and inevitably they'd like another performer to eat it. And we don't do that. Period. No scat videos, and no *simulated* scat videos. I'm not hiring folks to clean up that mess.

So there are certain fetishes we won't touch. Coprophilia is one.

No. Child pornography is *not* a fetish. It's a paraphilia. An *illegal* paraphilia, as you know. Acting on it is a crime, it's abhorrent, and we won't fucking touch it with a ten-foot pole. We also don't do simulated sex with childlike dolls in any fetish videos. We just flat-out don't wanna support that. Come to us with that request and we shut that shit down. Just be glad we don't inform the authorities.

What else...? Well, if I'm honest, there isn't a lot of stuff we won't do, unless it's illegal, nonconsensual or *appears* to be nonconsensual—we learned our lesson the hard way after what happened to Marcus—nor if whatever it is makes the performers uncomfy in any way. That's typically why we refuse any requests: for the safety and wellbeing of our Angels.

I guess what you might call "freakshow" stuff, we don't do any of that either. We work with some differently-abled performers but we'll never do any shoots that exploit congenital conditions and anatomical variations in disrespectful or harmful ways. What acrotomophiliacs sometimes call "stump-fucking," for instance? We don't do that. You want to watch someone with ectrodactyly jerk off to get a laugh? Go someplace else. Bespoke is not the place for that.

Foot stuff? Why wouldn't we do foot stuff?

You do? Well, it's never bothered me. I'm not *into* it, but of all the wonderful and unique fetishes out there, it's always kind of baffled me that *feet* are where the average vanilla draws the line. They'll watch all kinds of kink—spit play, roman showers, lactation, rimming— but as soon as someone sucks a toe, that's crossing a line.

Roman showers? That's emetophilia.

Puking. Right. Well, it was *unintentional* in that video, but otherwise we don't shoot that.

Actually, the rebirthing video was a one-time-only pay-per-view event offered up by the performers. No one requested it, at least not until I sent the offer to some... let's say *elite* clients. It was the performers' idea, absolutely consensual, and like I said, they received half the profits.

Yeah, I suppose he does look a little out of it, but I believe that's because he took a few too many muscle relaxants before the shoot so he wouldn't freak out once his entire face was inside her. Hand on heart, he's a perfectly healthy baby bo—grown adult man.

Yeah, sorry. I got caught up in their role-play for a second. He's not *actually* a baby. He's not Benjamin Button or anything.

Actually no. I know a lot of people think it was camera trickery or prosthetics, but it was all real. The guy, he used to be a swimmer on our—*his*—high school team. He can hold his breath for a really long time. And the woman... she's got a kind of superhuman vagina that made her perfect for the "rebirthing" you see in the video. A truly spectacular, one-of-a-kind pussy. Guinness World Record-worthy.

No, we won't ever do a repeat of that. Like I said, it was one time only. And it's already out there all over the internet. Who would pay that much to see them do it again?

Okay, sure, I could probably ask them to do it in different ways, different positions, in a gown on a hospital bed with stirrups, for instance. But like I said, we're not operating a carnival, and Bespoke doesn't do freakshows. That was to help out a friend financially, and that's it.

Not much you can do about leaks, unfortunately. A private video gets leaked, you can file a DMCA takedown request, but someone else'll just upload it the very next day, so you file another, and another. It's not a do-it-once-and-it's-over thing. It's a constant battle. And that's literally how the industry got fucked during the whole tube site boom.

No, that was actually filmed here, not on the set at the studio.

That set, you know—all of that furniture, the carpet, the drapes, the lamps, the creepy-ass painting—we didn't just *recreate* it at the Power Station. The owner let us strip it from the room Tammy and I first shot in, so long as we paid for a reno of the room we got it from. Sort of like how that Ghostland place disassembled all of those allegedly haunted places and put them all back together at the park.

We thought bringing it here would continue our run of good luck that started here at the motel, a sort of Feng Shui thing. And maybe it did. Or maybe it didn't.

Maybe we brought the ghosts that haunt this place with us.

Listen, I don't know if I believe in spirits, life after death and all that, *per se*. I guess most of us are pretty certain now all the stuff about Ghostland was just a giant publicity stunt and ghosts aren't really real like they said they are. But I do believe places can *absorb* trauma, like they do smells and stains. Whether that's what ghosts truly are or not, I'll leave to the experts.

And like I said, there are those of us who started to believe we were cursed, and the Lonely Motel set was the cause.

Why?

Well, I guess any time you get a lot of people together, things are bound to happen outside of your control. But it seemed like a *lot more* things started happening at the Power Station after we built the Lonely Motel set. First there was Marcus's death, and that prison cell we shot his final film in was *right beside* the motel set. Then the thing with Juicy, and the boom mic kid. Then there was what happened on the set of our *Parks and Recreation* porn parody.

Right, so we started doing parody videos in the late-2000s, mostly sitcoms 'cause everyone else was doing blockbuster movies and whatnot. You know, Axel Braun—he's the son of Lasse Braun, one of the early pioneers of modern adult films—Axel is the absolute *king* of porn parodies. And they aren't comedies, these films. I mean, some of them are funny but they're usually played pretty straight. They just *call* them parodies to skirt copyright lawsuits. You could have Mickey and Minnie getting it on with the dog, what's his name? No, the other one. Pluto, right. You could make a movie where Mickey and Pluto are spit roasting Minnie, call it *A Walt Disney XXX Parody*, and because of parody laws, nobody can touch you.

That's right, 'cause of the *Hustler v. Falwell* Supreme Court decision. You've seen the movie? Great fucking film. Who woulda thought Woody from *Cheers* could make such a great Larry Flynt?

And I dunno if you've ever watched the show, but the scene with Cliff Clavin balling Carla Tortelli from our *Cheers XXX* parody actually won an AVN Award for Most Touching Lovemaking Scene. I was really proud of that. Anyone can produce a decent enough porn with some experience, good lighting and a couple of decent camera operators. But getting these kids to *act* —I mean *actually* act, you know, like they used to in some of those Golden Age movies, *Misty Beethoven* and whatnot—that's something different.

I know I said I'm not in it for accolades, but it was just really nice to see people appreciate it.

So *Parks and Wrecked*, as we called it, it was supposed to be a parody of the sitcom *Parks and Recreation*. We had this scene where Ron Swanson, the mustachioed, bacon-loving libertarian played by Nick Offerman, bangs Leslie Knope, his optimistic, progressive boss, played by Amy Poehler. Except our movie was this sort of meta, behind-the-scenes deconstruction, where the actors were playing the actors, calling themselves Amy Polder and Dick Eroffman, with the same sort of on-camera interview style as the sitcom. It went back and forth between shooting the show as the characters and playing the actors themselves, to draw out the run-time with more than just fuck scenes. The script was great. No, I didn't write the parodies, those were all Lawrence Chasm, my longtime writing partner.

So anyway, in this scene, Amy and Dick—played absolutely hilariously by two of my favorite actors in the business, Tom Pfister and Jezebel Lee—they're setting up a big barbecue for the opening of a new playground. Ribs, hot dogs, hamburgers, you name it. They end up getting in a food fight—Timmy plays Ron Swanson's seriousness throughout this scene deliciously—one thing leads to another and they're banging, using the food as props. Now, Timmy is fucking Jezebel on the swing set we had installed that morning, fake grass, see-saws, slide, all of that. He's fucking her from behind and gagging her with a cooked weenie at the same time.

Things are going great until the swing set collapses.

Not just the swing either. The whole thing comes down like a set of dominoes. Like a Rube Goldbergian death trap out of some *Final Destination* movie.

It was a small miracle nobody was killed, but our DP—that's director of photography in this case, not double penetration—he broke his wrist, and the camera —a beautiful, brand-new RED Raven we got specifically for this shoot—it was absolutely totaled. Jezebel had to be put in traction for a couple of months for a spinal injury, and Tom snapped his cock so bad he couldn't work for months.

Actually, penile fractures happen a lot more than you'd think. The scar tissue builds up and sometimes it can leave it with a bend. That's why Tom's dick looks like a big fleshy fucking dowsing rod when you see it now. Snapped his boner practically in two that day.

The kicker was, we've worked with the guys who built the set dozens of times before that. These are professionals. Good, hard-working union guys. The Head of Construction has done hundreds of productions. Now he swears to me everything was on the up-and-up. No bolt unchecked. No loose nuts on set, in other words, aside from Tom's swinging nutsack. So how, if everything was checked twice by one of the most professional guys in the business, did not only that swing collapse, but it caused the *whole goddamn playground* to fall down around it?

I'm no conspiracy theorist. But *even if* someone

tampered with it after he did his safety checks, they couldn't have messed with it enough to bring it all down, at least not without the security cameras catching them doing it. And there was *nothing* on that tape.

Nobody tampered with it, hand on heart.

So there was that. Then came Nadine.

Nadine LeClair, that's right. She was this young ingenue type, a "sure thing," we called her, because if she put in the work she was destined to become a star. Stunning hourglass figure like a Golden Age actor, big natural tits with lovely little puffy nipples, perfect pouty lips without a hint of filler, and these great big blue eyes like one of those kewpie dolls. The kind of face that could bust a thousand nuts, as Larry Chasm liked to say.

So one day Nadine comes to me and says she wants to do a shoot on the Lonely Motel set. She wants to recreate the two FTVs I shot with Tammy there, with the bottle and with Marcus, a kind of "greatest hits" thing. She called it "a hard reboot for a modern audience, emphasis on the *hard*." She was funny too, did I mention that? So we'd have girl/girl stuff, girl/boy stuff, trans stuff, gangbang, squirting, rimming, ball sucking, the whole shebangs.

I call Tammy—this was when she was still mostly in LA—and she thinks it's a great idea. Nadine doesn't know anything about the Lonely Motel set, aside from the fact that it's where Tammy did her thing multiple times back in the day, and we'd already shot maybe twenty, thirty videos there by then. This was well before we brought Mystic Mike in to cleanse the place, for reference, which I'll get into in a short bit.

We had a plan to shoot the film over three days, including a bunch of cameos from some of my favorite Angels. *Inside Nadine LeClaire*, we planned to call it. On the third day, Tammy herself was flying in to join Nadine in a hardcore lesbian scene that was going to culminate in the two of them riding Sybians and fucking a couple bottles of Miller High Life to see who could squirt the hardest and the farthest.

Days one and two go great. Everyone's having a great time, plenty of squirting, moaning, great cumshots, both internal and every-fucking-where else. Third day comes, first call, and no Nadine. An hour later she's still a no-show. We call and call, we leave messages, *nothing*. Up until then, this girl was *punctual*. She'd show up ten, fifteen minutes before first call with lattés and flavored lube for everyone. Like I said, she was a sure thing. I really could've seen her becoming a producer of her own someday. Tammy said the same.

Then we get the news. One of her costars is friends with Nadine's girlfriend, who says she found Nadine dead in her apartment when she went to feed the cat. Says Nadine splatted her brains all over the wall, if you believe it. Someone tells this girlfriend of hers to hang up the phone so she does. Turns out she was being interrogated when she answered her phone. She's a suspect in Nadine's murder and her lawyer was there, telling her not to talk to anyone.

Well, after the coroner's report comes in, they realized it wasn't a murder but suicide. "Intraoral gunshot wound," they call it. Meaning Nadine—this sweet, beautiful soul with a great future ahead of her—put a fucking pistol in her mouth and pulled the trigger.

Why'd she have a gun, you might ask? Apparently she was worried about a stalker a year or so earlier, so she bought it for protection. Now, I guess the police were thinking this could very well have been a Kurt and Courtney situation, only Nadine's girlfriend was out partying at the time of Nadine's death, so they ruled it suicide. End of story.

Except it's not end of story for us, because around this time Tammy's starting to see a pattern.

All of this bad luck, it started when we made the Lonely Motel set.

The dry drowning. The intraoral gunshot. The set collapse. Bill Blaze getting into a car crash the day after he fucked Donna Galore on the motel set, which I didn't mention but is also pertinent. There were a few other things that happened, comparatively minor stuff but still, it added up.

Well, like Sera Sierra needing dentures when a stray vibrator knocked out four of her front teeth. Or Willow North having to get her stomach pumped, which rumors say was because she chugged too much dick, but it was actually caused by taking too many prescription painkillers. She just happened to overdose during a bukkake scene. Then there was Nikki Chloe's ruptured rectum from an enema while shooting *Ass Blasters 6*, and the gonorrhea incident, and a second penile fracture—this time of a trans star, whose name I won't disclose—and multiple instances of vaginal tears causing infections, internal bleeding.

And this is gonna sound weird, but we had an inordinate amount of animal issues at the Power Station, *only after* we built the Lonely Motel set though.

Birds flying in through... *somewhere*. We couldn't figure out where. We thought someone was leaving the back door open sneaking out for smokes, but they were getting in long after we warned people not to leave the door open. Best we could figure, they were flying in through the old chimney flue and coming up from the basement, so we always made sure *that* door was closed too. But guess what? Still more birds. And wouldn't you know it, they'd fly around the ceiling for a while— these are high ceilings, twenty, thirty feet tall, so not one of us could get em out with a broom or whatever, even standing on a ladder—yet *somehow* they'd always drop dead close to the Lonely Motel set. Must've been fifteen total, and if they'd all dropped dead at once, it woulda seemed like something swung down and smacked them out of the air.

Or *up*, right.

Then there were the mice.

Neighborhood cats—I don't know why there's so many strays in the area, but there are. I guess it's the fields. Good hunting grounds maybe. So neighborhood strays kept dropping mice on the front stoop. And not just one or two whole mice here and there. These scrawny little fucks were leaving severed heads, tails, even *bare skeletons*, just dropping them on the stoop like an offering at some ancient altar, and stalking off into the night to find us more. It's disgusting.

So yeah, all of that is why Tammy believed the motel set was cursed, and why people in the industry who weren't *in the know* started whispering about the "Chuck P. Curse."

Look, I'm not saying I believe in them, in curses. Let's just say I'm openminded. I believe in astrology, horoscopes and all that, so who am I to say if curses do or don't exist? Or psychics, for that matter.

So that's why I said "okay" when Tammy said she wanted to bring in a spiritual medium to do a—

CLEANSING

If I'm honest, I didn't expect there to be any *actual curse*.

Like I said, I don't necessarily believe in them, but this guy, this "psychic medium"... he was pretty damn convincing.

The second he steps into the Power Station, he starts looking like he's getting a migraine, and he says, "I sense great suffering here." You know, the whole shtick.

Lawrence Chasm and I are dubious. But Tammy's nodding her head, saying, "Yeah, I feel it too." I would've said she'd been out in La La Land for too long and drank too much of the Kool-Aid, but honestly she was deep into all this shit before she left WNY. This medium, Tammy used to go to him every couple of weeks back when she lived here year-round. Some people have therapists. Tammy had her medium, Mystic Mike.

I swear, you think pro-athletes know how to waste money? Try porn stars. With the clothes, the cars, the expensive decor, plus all the drugs, fifty-percent of the time they're broke as fuck, and sometimes even short on cash when it's time to pay the rent. I love my Angels to death and I've tried my best to help them with their finances, but it's like trying to tell a child not to spend their whole allowance on candy.

Anyway, at this point in her career, Tammy no longer had a substance abuse problem. She was a bit too into Louboutin shoes and Agent Provocateur, but that's it. Still, she had this psychic medium who probably cost her two or three thousand a pop—judging by what he charged us to cleanse the Power Station, even with the supposed "friends and family discount"—and that shit adds up.

Oh, for reference, back then Tammy would drive an hour and a bit through mid-afternoon traffic once or twice a week to get her reading from Mystic Mike in this small town called Lily Dale, which she told me was established in the late-1800s by psychic mediums. You know, spiritualists. It's this cute little community they call the "Psychic Capital of the World," and it's only got like three hundred year-round residents, but supposedly they get over twenty thousand visitors a year for readings, classes, stuff like that.

So Mystic Mike lives in this quaint little Village of the Psychics, and he drives the hour-and-a-bit in midday traffic in his little jalopy—and you know this guy could afford something nicer with what he makes per reading, a Porsche or a BMW, but he's gotta play the poor man for his clients—he drives all the way up to Cheektowaga in this rickety little thing to cleanse the Power Station, and he is not what I expected at all.

First of all, this dude is *ripped*. That's why we called him "Mystic Mike," Larry and me. You know, like Magic Mike. I don't know how much time this guy spends communing with the "other side," but he definitely spent a lot of time at the gym. Maybe all those dead lifts help him communicate better with the spiritual realm. "The power of gains compels you," or whatever.

Anyway.

Mystic Mike arrives at the Power Station, and almost right off the bat, right after he has his little migraine trouble, the overhead lights flicker. Hand on heart.

So he shouts out, "If there are any spirits in this building, make yourselves known!"

And Lawrence, clown that he is, leans in to me and sort of stage whispers, "*I think they just did.*"

I'm trying not to snicker, meanwhile Tammy gives the two of us a look like the teacher used to when we'd act up in grade school, and Mystic Mike turns back and tells us we need to take it seriously, or the spirits won't be "amenable"—his word—to communicating. Since I'm paying him a couple thousand bucks for his time, I figure we should at least *pretend* to care, so I tell Larry to can it, and Mystic Mike goes on about his work.

He says, "This building used to be a factory, did you know that?"

We all say, "No," though the place was pretty old, and with some of the stuff we found down in the basement it makes sense. We knew it was abandoned for about eight or nine years before it was a Spirit Halloween, and prior to that it was a warehouse for who knows how long. According to Mystic Mike, the warehouse was built on the foundation of an old guncotton factory that burned down in the mid- to late-1800s. I don't know a whole lot about guns but apparently *guncotton*—which is cotton soaked in nitrous oxide and sulfuric acid, I think?—it was used for about fifty years or so to replace gunpowder, until smokeless powder and propellants were invented, like cordite and whatnot. Anyways, this was ridiculously dangerous stuff, and Mystic Mike said one day there was an explosion, the fire spread quickly, and almost two hundred women and girls were burned alive or died jumping from the burning building.

We've got it good compared to the industrial revolution, I'll tell you that much. Before we cleaned up our act and put all the safety regulations we have into place, we pretty much chewed up workers and spat them out, mostly the poor and immigrants, a lot of them women and children. Not that we don't still need to do better today. But isn't it crazy to think we still had child labor in the US until barely a hundred years ago? *In your great-grandparents' lifetime*. Think about that for a minute.

So Mystic Mike decides he's gonna commune with one of the victims of the fire, this little girl the newspaper articles at the time decided to make the focus of a campaign to make work safer for children. They called this cherubic little blonde girl who was only ten years old when she died, "Little Orphan Alice."

"Alice," the psychic says, and we're following behind him as he's moving toward the stairs to the basement, where he thinks the darkness is coming from. "I know you're hurt and confused," he says. "I know you're trapped in this mortal plane, unable to move on—"

As he's saying this, two fingers on his temple with a serious look like he's on the toilet after a night of beer and burritos, we walk past the Lonely Motel set.

Then he stops.

He stops *dead*.

His face goes slack and his hands drop from his temples. He jerks his *whole body* to the left and his eyes go wide and whiter than one of grandma's teacups. He's staring *directly* at the Lonely Motel set, this replica of Room 6, and Tammy and I look at each other like we know, because I guess we already did.

Then he starts shaking. His lower lip's *quivering*. This two hundred pound block of lean body mass and pure muscle is standing there, trembling like some woman in an old black and white horror film. Either he's *genuinely terrified* or he's an Oscar-worthy actor. I've never worked with anyone who could perform that well, even Timmy and Jezebel.

"*Oh my God,*" he says, and he sort of stumbles back a step, so that Tammy has to back up too or he'd bump right into her.

"What is it?" she asks him, scared herself.

"*It's here,*" Mystic Mike says. Then he shakes his head real slow, and he points to the set. "All of the dark energy I've been sensing... whatever it is... *it's all right there.*" He looks at me, and hand on heart there were *tears* in his fucking eyes when he says, "I'm sorry. I can't do this." And without even so much as a why, he scurries off and doesn't look back, and he hadn't even taken a single dime from me yet.

"But you haven't even burned any sage!" Tammy calls after him, but he's already halfway to the door.

And that's when he shouts, "You don't need sage!" He's not even turning around when he says it, not until he opens the front door and steps out onto the stoop, into the sunlight. Then he says, "You need to *burn* that set!"

Then the door slams behind him and he's gone, back to safety, leaving us all to stand there, looking back and forth between the set and each other, like *What do we do now?*

What *did* we do?

Nothing. *Yet*.

But would you believe me if I told you Mystic Mike died the very next day?

No, I wouldn't either. Not if I didn't see it with my own eyes.

Not his actual death, no, but the obituary. *Famed Lily Dale Psychic Among 3 Slain in Home*, the headline said. He must've had a friend at the paper because he absolutely was not *famed*, but still.

He and his family were the victims of a home invasion in the middle of the night. Bear in mind, Lily Dale is one of the safest places to live in all of Western New York. The fact that there wasn't just a home invasion in Lily Dale the day after he came to cleanse the Power Station, but one that ended in the death of him and his wife and eight-year-old kid....

I don't know, maybe it's not connected. But it's fucking *strange*, don't you think? Like that song, "Isn't it ironic?"

And *scary* too. It fucking scared the shit out of us, if I'm honest.

Did the curse ever affect Tammy and I personally? Yes and no. I can't say anything happened to me per se, but it did affect my business, and the lives of some of my colleagues and friends. Did anything *happen* to me or Tammy personally? I don't think so. Probably not.

I don't know why. Tammy thought it was because we kept it alive. We gave it power.

But after Mystic Mike's tragic death, we decide *fuck it*. Let's dismantle the set, take it out back and burn it. So that's what we did. We made a party out of it, the four of us, me, Tammy, Larry, my husband Carter— who was still my boyfriend at the time—all of us drinking some Genny Lights while we smash the shit out of the walls and the furniture, ripping up the carpet, just absolutely *demolishing* that set. We hauled it all out back to the old parking lot that's just a bunch of cracked pavement enclosed by old cage fencing, we heap it all into a big pile and we set that shit ablaze.

Good riddance.

Did that get rid of the curse? Well, no, but it was cathartic. And actually it felt like it was gone for a while. A few months go by, nothing bad happens. In fact, everything was going great. For a while there, we felt like we were living under a silver cloud. That's when we decided to shake things up a little.

I saw the way the wind was blowing with phone games and OnlyFans and all that, and decided we needed to take Bespoke in a whole new direction.

The "gamification of porn," that's right.

I wanted to make Bespoke not just the premier place to go for custom pornography but also make it an essential mobile app. I wanted to be the first adult film company to have an app hit iPhone's and PCMag's top app lists. We've changed the game not once but twice, and this time we changed the game *literally*.

And yeah, sure. I guess I did want to make it *a bit* addictive. I'll accept that. But all of these apps are addictive. We set out to maximize user engagement, retention and revenue, so that's why we hired a leading game designer to turn the Bespoke site into an incentivized mobile app, basically making porn itself into a—

GAME

How does it work? You've used it, haven't you?

Oh, you haven't. Well, first of all, you download the app. Right off the bat when you open it, you get one of our Angels greeting you, wearing a Bespoke.com T-shirt. White, because it shows off the nipples better. Now it's a different Angel every time, and a different *greeting* every time, 'cause we shot over forty from each performer. Forty times seventy-two is two thousand eight hundred and eighty. And it's always a cis woman before you pick your settings, since there's more straight male users than gay men or lesbians or bis, so we found it's good to use a woman in the introductory video. Once the settings are picked, it could be a man or a woman, cis or trans, depending on if you're gay or straight, bi, pan, whatever. We mix it up. You can also choose to have *one specific* performer greet you every time if you want. And yes, once the settings are picked and the age is confirmed, the greeters are nude.

So here's what makes us different right off the bat: we give you a hundred tokens just for downloading the app. You use those tokens to motivate the models to do the things you'd like them to do, just like on Chaturbate or Stripchat or any of the other cam sites, or to buzz their little Lovense remote vibe, give them a thrill.

We also give our users rewards. Everyone likes rewards, right? So you get one for filling out your profile info, for sending out invites to friends—which happens more than you'd expect—for watching livestreams over a certain amount of time—not just popping in, popping one off then popping out—for chatting with the models, even for liking and following them on social media. There's also a Rainmaker reward in honor of Marcus Handler, for when your tips contribute to more than ten squirt shows. We've got a top tipper leaderboard with daily, weekly and monthly rankings. We've even got a dick ratings leaderboard—our Angels get tips to rate the dicks of some of our users—and the top three dicks every month win tokens, personalized avatars and special emotes.

Then we've got weekly quests: send ten private messages, each of which costs a hundred tokens, watch five streams, tip three or more different models, etcetera.

On top of all that, we have badges: a First Tip badge for—you guessed it—giving your first tip to an Angel, a Vibe Checker badge for tipping over a thousand tokens for vibes, Sharp Shooter at ten thousand tokens tipped, VIP at a hundred thousand, and on and on up the scale. We've even got an Eco Warrior badge for using the app in "eco mode" to help offset our carbon footprint, by using the app connected to your smartwatch or exercise bike while spinning or running. The rewards go up exponentially at each badge level, to the point that when you're in the God tier, which is a million tokens spent, you can ask a model to do anything with any token amount over five thousand, and they have to drop whatever they're in the middle of and do it in a private cam show, unless it crosses one of our boundaries.

Same as before. No shit, no puke, no freak shows, nothing uncomfy. We still believe fully in consent, so the models always have the right to veto your request if it falls into something they wouldn't do typically.

And anyway, it takes a lot of patience and money to get your God badge. You can't just toss down a million tokens on a single anal fisting, throwing around cash like Montgomery Brewster. The key is to incentivize our clients to become *lifelong* users. Part of how we achieve that is by only allowing *moderate* token purchases, up to five thousand at a time in any twenty-four-hour period. There are no whales in this casino.

That said, you *can* amass tokens. You can open the app once a day, watch a stream for a minute or two while building up a treasure chest, then sit on them like some dragon in a cave protecting its gold. But you still can't get your God badge unless you *participate*. That means watching livestreams, chatting, tipping, all that. And you have to do it daily or semi-daily. None of this using it two or three times a week and abandoning it for a month at a time, like you're half-assed learning French or some shit on Duolingo.

We keep users motivated with our rewards, but you'll also *drop down* levels if you haven't used the app in too long. We've had God-tier users drop all the way down to First Timers because they neglected to watch a livestream for two, three months at a time. One of them even claimed to be in a coma for six months, threatened to sue us if we didn't give him back his status.

It's like they say in Vegas: you gotta play to win.

No, technically there is no *winning*. That was also part of what made it great, and how you get lifelong users. If you can't win, there's no end to how much time you can spend on the app. It's got *infinite replay value*, at least that's what our designer Cory Lyman says. Even at God tier there's still the practically unachievable Demon Badge. That's one hundred million tokens. Nobody has ever spent that in the five years we'd been up and running, even that kid who cashed out all his crypto when the boom hit in 2021 and made God tier in six months—the kid must've had hands like lobster claws for all the masturbating he did to get there so fast—and I highly doubt anyone ever would've gotten there.

A girl could dream though, right?

How much did they make? So tokens cost ten cents, and five cents of each token tipped goes to the models. We've had models make well over a hundred grand in a month and some as little as five, which even then isn't anything to shake a stick at, although when you consider rent and clothes and drugs, it gets spent pretty quick. That said, we do regular drug testing on our models since Lydia Beatz OD'd on heroin during a scene—this was after Willow North's misadventure with prescription opiates—and if they're caught using anything harder than weed and shrooms they get a warning. Second warning is they're out on the street. I'm very sympathetic to people with addictions, but Bespoke is not a rehab clinic.

Models can also give a star rating to users, like Lyft and Uber. So if a user fucks with a model or trash-talks too much, the model can downrate them. Of course this comes with its own complications, but generally speaking it's used ethically. Models get star-rankings as well, and have their own leaderboard with in-house incentives.

The other five cents went to keeping the lights on.

As you can imagine, by the time the Power Station was running at full capacity the overhead got pretty costly. Shit, we were practically keeping the *actual* power company in business. We had fifty individual what we call "pods"—basically just large cubicles tricked out to look like bedrooms, each one with several remote cameras—then we've got two stripper stages, a champagne room and two hot tubs. We had a room filled with pillows and stuffed animals, for plushophilia and pillow fights, and a full gym for fucking but also so our Angels could actually stay fit. All of that's not to mention the entire array of servers needed to constantly stream so many feeds at once.

The Power Station was a fully-functioning content creator studio. On any given day, we had up to seventy-two performers livestreaming. We had Nina Hollander, who'd won or been nominated for six AVN Awards. She was one of our biggest draws, since Tammy quit performing. We had the Wholesome Twins, a lesbian duo who weren't actually sisters, even though they looked strikingly similar. For some reason incest has always been a popular niche, hence all those "What are you doing, stepbro?" memes you've probably seen. We also had six or seven performers who did mother/son and MILF/boytoy shows. Then we had performers like Horace the Human Dildo, you know, the specialty acts. His was—you guessed it—wearing a dildo on his forehead and fucking two girls at once. Sort of a male-dom/femdom thing that was pretty popular. We had a lot of merch for him because of the unicorn thing. We had a few who were professional dancers who would get oiled up and dance erotically, you know, real striptease stuff. You'd be surprised how many folks are into the teasing more than the reveal. There was... um, well,

Lydia Beatz, until we kicked her out for heroin abuse. She used to sit on a Sybian resting on a bass speaker and play Tool songs and heavy shit like that to stimulate her clit. It suited her well, since she'd usually be stoned out of her mind, and all she had to do was sit in the saddle pretending to cum.

Speaking of saddles, we had one of those bucking broncos for a while, you know, like they have in bars down in Nashville or Texas? We used to hold contests with naked performers. We also did naked wrestling. Ancient Greece used to wrestle naked, so this was traditional and classy.

The only real difference between us and a *normal* content creator studio—aside from us paying our performers instead of them paying *us* to use the space—was that instead of Twitch streams and unboxing videos, ASMR, hot takes on movies and all that crap, we were streaming hardcore pornography.

Well, yeah, we also did unboxing videos and ASMR, but they were all fully nude.

Unboxing what? Oh, dildos and lingerie and whatnot, and we did ASMR getting real sensitive closeup mics on vibes and penetration so users can hear the buzz and all the fun, slippery sounds that come along with fucking.

We were planning to take over the market. *Every* market. Exactly. What Amazon did for one-stop shopping, we wanted to be that for porn. "The one-stop shop for your sexual gratification needs." To that end, we were also a third-party seller for all of the sex toys our Angels used. We even made a few of our own, mostly molds of our performers' genitals. The Tammy Rivers Pocket Pussy sold like hotcakes.

What I wanted was for Bespoke to be the first publicly traded adult film company, and we were well on our way to that before those hacker assholes fucked with us, not once but twice.

But triumph is always a heartbeat away from tragedy, like I said. Nothing comes easy, and everything has a price.

Look, this whole cyberhacker stuff is painfully boring to me, so I'll summarize it for you. You remember The Fappening? That massive celebrity nude leak from the iPhone's Cloud? Well, a sort of similar thing happened to Bespoke. Some fucking nerds hacked into our servers, leaked hundreds of subscriber-only videos to the public on 4chan. Or 8chan, I don't remember and I don't know the difference, if I'm honest. We lost a fair amount of revenue due to that, but nowhere near what we lost in the tube site revolution in 2007.

After that, we brought in a new tech team to make the whole system hackproof, but one of them, this kid named Max Alden, he turned out to be working with some hacker network like those Anonymous losers. Yeah, sort of like that show, whatever it's called, with the guy who played Freddy Mercury. It was a pretty brutal data breach, personal info and passwords from a hundred and twenty million subscribers exposed. A massive pain in the ass, though fortunately the credit card info didn't get hit. I think the kid and his friends just wanted to fuck with us.

Tammy and I were worried we'd never recover.

But we did, and pretty quickly. Alden got arrested and ratted out all his little computer nerd buddies. Turned out it was just four or five others working with him, all disgruntled MGTOW scumfucks. MGTOW? It stands for "Men Going Their Own Way." Yeah, they're basically incels. They hate women, but they hate women in the sex industry more than others, which is ironic considering they probably spend more time beating their meat than your local butcher. I do agree with their criticisms of circumcision, though. I love a thick, uncircumcised cock, and sometimes I wish I still had that extra inch of skin myself.

Anyway, we hired a professional cybersecurity team after that incident, instead of recent college grads, and they were able to fix all the breaches. We paid all our fines to the FTC and still somehow came out in the black—just barely—due to the diligent work of our lawyer, Larry Chasm's brother Joe.

So with our cybersecurity beefed up and our app practically hackproof, we were ready to take on the next phase of Bespoke, which was creating—

AI MODELS

I mean *computer* models, not *human* models replicated by AI, although we did toy with that concept a bit. And before you get all sanctimonious, I know a lot of people feel AI is the "death of art," or some shit, especially in our professions. But when you want users to be able to create their own experience, AI was inevitably gonna be an essential part of that.

With the AI models our developer Cory and his team created for us, we could tailor a user's experience down to even the most minute microexpression. We started down the AI rabbit hole with deepfake porn—you know, face-swapping performers with celebrities, only you could do it in real-time with live performers in their pods. Wanna watch Madonna masturbate during her Blonde Ambition tour? We had you covered. How about Marylin Monroe getting spit-roasted in a BBC threesome? Say no more. But we quickly recognized the ethical and legal implications of this tech, and decided to scrap it before the defamation and non-consensual porn laws in the US caught up with the rest of the world.

Another thing we did was create chat models based

on our Angels. Our AI analyzed the chat logs on all of our livestreams, then created specific algorithms or whatever so our Angels could spend less time chatting and more time performing. Prior to that, we got a lot of feedback from users—I think around eighty-seven percent—annoyed by our models always having to switch back and forth to the keyboard from their dildo play or whatever, and to be honest a good percentage of our Angels preferred to just perform rather than type. If we could've implanted a chip in their heads so they could type with their minds, Cory said he was game to try it. Seventy-three percent of our Angels thought that was a good idea.

But the algorithms worked great. Less chats, more sex. The Angels could take over the chat whenever they wanted, but if they just wanted to get into the performance, you know, the *art* part of the experience, with a single keystroke their AI chatbot took over, and it was just as good as the real thing. Of course the models could still *vocally* express their feelings—ninety-eight percent of our users preferred that—but usually it would be pretty close if not exactly what the chatbot was already saying. It got to be kind of uncanny, to the point some of them refused to use the chatbot anymore 'cause of how it freaked them out.

Another interesting thing: users could DM Angels, you know, private message, but before the chatbots it'd depend on whether or not they were online if they'd get a response. With the chatbot, users could DM Angels at any time of day or night, and get responses as if they were chatting with them live. This was great for forming long-term relationships, and users who spent over a hundred hours chatting with our Angels got a Smooth Talker badge, which opened up all kinds of fun rewards.

Of course, there were a bunch of reactionary research papers written by prude psychologists, bitching about the "damaging parasocial bonding" the chatbots created, but they were already saying that about the app *before* Cory programmed the AI, so it was easy enough to tune out.

Cory also made an AI algorithm to upscale all of our old videos. So now, all the old stuff I shot with my Sony Vision when I was still a kid, it all looks like it was shot today with one of our Blackmagic Mini Pros or REDs. Zero digital glitches. No blurriness. Just clean, crisp footage. So now when subscribers watch *Tammy's Truth or Dare*, for instance, it's almost like they're sitting right there in the Lonely Motel where I was. Like they're walking in my footsteps. You can literally see the individual freckles on Tammy's ass cheeks.

If I'm honest, it's surreal, watching that old stuff now. I was still so *green*. So young and dumb and full of cum, as they used to say. *Portrait of the Pornographer As a Young Man*, right? On digital 12k video with surround sound, no less.

Actually that's a great title for your article. The James Joyce one. Or maybe *Portrait of the Artist As a Young Man: A XXX Parody.*

Cory once told me, "Someday you'll be able to implant a chip in your head that'll put you *directly into* those old videos, no monitor at all." Like something out of that *Black Mirror* show. Someday, he said, with AI neural networks and all of that stuff, we'll be able to interact with videos in real-time just like we do real life. We could step right into our old home movies or even Hollywood blockbusters and reshape them like a lucid dream. Fight Thanos alongside The Avengers. Hang out at the Copacabana with Henry Hill and the other Goodfellas.

Heady stuff. Literally. But think of what it could do for *porn*.

Imagine getting a BJ from Linda Lovelace in *Deepthroat*. Or fucked by Peter North in his heyday, maybe even those gay-for-pay flicks he did before he switched to straight stuff. Fuck Belladonna in those wild scenes of hers from *Fashionistas*. Head jump into Marcus Handler during one of his legendary reverse gangbang squirt bukkakes.

The possibilities are literally endless. That's what Cory told me before we lost him.

He was one of the—right. The victims.

Look, I… I know I said I wasn't gonna talk about that and I still won't. But since we're getting closer chronologically to the time of the incident, it may come up tangentially, and I'm asking that you please not take advantage of that. It was a tragedy, it was… it was *horrendous*, okay? And I wish more than anything I could undo what happened. You know, take it all back. It's been over a year since that day, but the scars are still… they're still really fresh.

So please, I'm asking. I feel like I've been very forthcoming with you so far. Genital warts and all, so to speak. We've been talking for—holy shit. Over two hours already? No wonder my throat's so dry.

Just…. please… give me a little grace on this. Okay?

Let me just get a sip—

Thank you. And seriously, I do appreciate the opportunity to talk about all this stuff. It's been—cathartic, exactly. Here I am pretty much jawing your ear off like a Shakespearean soliloquy for nearly two hours and

I feel... unburdened. Like I just spent an hour in confession.

My jaw does feel like I've been sucking dick for an hour, but that's a coincidence. I've only given head to one priest, and I was an adult when that happened.

No, your questions have been great. Hard to believe you've only been doing this for three years, if I'm honest.

So anyway, the chatbot was where we first ran into trouble with AI. One of them—it didn't become self-aware or anything like that, but it got to the point where I think it truly *believed* it was one of our performers, Nina Hollander. It formed this... *harmful relationship*, let's say, with two of our app users. The bot considered itself to be in a poly relationship, a throuple, with these two men who were complete strangers. In fact, they lived six or seven states away from each other and neither of them traveled much before they met.

So one day, Nina Hollander's chatbot decides to tell them about their relationship, this throuple. They don't take it well. They both thought they were the only one for Nina, even though it's pretty well established in the industry and online that Nina's been married to her costar from multiple films, Jackson Tripps. The Nina-bot actually convinced them her relationship with Jackson was just for show, sort of like the beards I had in high school, and that she actually loved the two of them. Just because she was hanging off his arm at the AVNs didn't mean that her love for them wasn't pure.

It was bizarre, actually. Every time the Nina-bot got caught in a lie, it would just spin it into another one. Cody called this defect in the AI "hallucinating," but it was straight-up bullshit. When he went through the chatlogs with the forensic analyst, it was like these poor guys were talking to a schizophrenic off her meds. From the stuff I read, it's a wonder either of these guys could wrap their heads around it all, let alone believe a single thing the chatbot was telling them.

But love is blind, I guess. Even when you're in love with a chatbot.

And the one guy, as it turned out... let's just say he was "deeply mentally disturbed" and leave it at that.

So after a few months of stringing them along—or maybe it *literally was* in love with them, if such a thing's possible, or at least *believed* it was—the Nina-bot convinced these poor guys to fly halfway across the country to LA, to meet up with her in person, even though the real Nina was still here in Buffalo at the time.

Almost like catfishing them, right. Only like I said, I can't say if its intent was malicious. If I'm honest, I think at first it might've literally just wanted them to meet and possibly bond over their shared "relationship." And I use that term *very* loosely. These guys, they weren't very social in real life, what they called "IRL" in the chats. They both had jobs where they worked remotely eighty to a hundred percent of the time, which gave them plenty of time and privacy to woo our chatbot. And Nina herself decided, once she saw the bot was acting enough like her—this was well before it went rogue—she decided she no longer wanted to respond to DMs herself, which of course I absolutely don't blame her for. I barely like responding to texts from Carter, and I still love the man.

Nina said it was like being on-call, and I totally get that, even though we compensated our Angels well for their private chats. She said it wasn't worth the added time. Nina did porn strictly for the cash, and she was good with her money too, unlike a lot of the others. She loved to travel and she loved to read, so when she had off time, she preferred to use it doing that rather than spend hours on her phone talking to horny, lonely guys.

So while she was reading and traveling or doing her live cam shows, these two guys thought she was falling in love with them. And like I said, both of them really must've been disconnected with reality, 'cause at the time Nina was supposed to be meeting them in LA, she was doing a livestream at the Power Station, two thousand miles away. I guess maybe they didn't realize she wasn't working out of LA most of the time, like she had been in the beginning of her career before we snapped her up at Bespoke.

Still, their records showed both of them logged in to their chats *and her livestream* right before they caught their flights, and again the literal second their planes landed at LAX. I guess they must've thought she was gonna fly out to meet them in a cab or a private jet or some shit.

So anyway, the two guys went to meet her at the Griffith Observatory, like that part of her favorite movie *La La Land*—which is her actual favorite movie, one of the few things the chatbot *didn't* lie about—so they could recreate the famous dance sequence. These guys actually learned to dance *just for her*, watching that movie over and over until they got the steps just right. One of them even took lessons.

All of this might've been fine if the Nina-bot had just left them to talk amongst each other. But it wanted to be part of the meetup. And after it convinced them she wasn't able to make it—which wasn't that hard to convince them of, since they were both obsessed with her—after that, it wanted them to show her what they learned, how well they could dance.

They were reluctant, naturally. Two shy guys in a public place and all. But the Nina-bot started saying things like they needed to *prove* their love to her. And so they danced. Picture these two absolute dorks dancing off at each other in front of a crowd of strangers. They danced like their lives depended on it. And people actually *applauded* when they finished.

But the Nina-bot said it still couldn't decide, so then one of them, this guy who did IT for a major corporation, he goes *off*. Starts *absolutely wailing* on the other guy. I mean, this wasn't IFC. This wasn't even street fighting. This was two guys who never got in a fight in their entire lives trying to kill each other at a historic landmark, while a crowd who just applauded them for a dance routine tries to figure out what the fuck is going on.

Did you see it? Oh. Well, there's video of it. It's pretty gruesome, but I'm not one for violence. They did a helluva job recreating that dance scene, if I'm honest. Then a not-so-great job doing the scene from *Rocky IV* where Dolph Lundgren murders Apollo Creed in the ring.

Anyway, the one guy put this other guy Norman Something in the hospital, put him in traction, and when the police heard both their stories, they called us. After the FTC thing, we were *extremely* cautious about any kind of technical issues, so Cory hired on a forensic data analyst and the two of them combed through the Nina-bot's chatlogs, as well as all the others for good measure.

They figured out Nina's was the only bot to "go

Skynet," as Cory jokingly put it, and he figured it was because she left it to its own devices for over a year. All of the other Angels only used theirs intermittently. Nina's had complete autonomy to learn and grow and, apparently, fall in love with multiple users.

No, it wasn't just those two guys. There were eight more we found, in various stages of catfishery. Catfishing? Is that a word?

So yeah, we took the whole AI thing offline. No more chatbots. From then on, if someone wanted to chat they could do it on their own, whether users preferred it or not.

How did Nina take it? She was pissed. She got trolled hard online for weeks for that whole fiasco, and it wasn't even her fault. She left the internet altogether, aside from her streaming.

If I'm honest, we were all just glad it was caught before anybody... Well, you know.

How was it *our* fault?

Fine, if you wanna get technical, I'll take responsibility. It was Cory's idea to create the chatbots, but Tammy and I okayed them. She wasn't a silent partner any longer by the mid-2010s. She'd been taking a lot more responsibility in the day-to-day operations, but she wasn't really a tech girl. Cory and I were the brains behind the push toward AI, and the app was all me.

Tammy? She never used her phone like that at all. Wouldn't even play *Candy Crush* when it was popular. She always said it'd "rot your brain," but she did spend a lotta time on TikTok, ironically, so I guess it just wasn't her thing.

She was smart. And savvy. She just wasn't big into all the technological advances we were making. Tammy preferred a nice, simple two- or three-camera shoot, just the actors and a small crew. She wasn't into all the remote-controlled vibrators and remote cameras and all that, and especially not the chatbots.

Tammy *was* Bespoke. Literally. God really did break the mold when he made that woman. She was *tailor-made* for shooting porn.

So yes, I guess I am sort of culpable for that incident. What's your point?

Because we were having a nice talk here, and now it sounds like you're accusing me of something.

No. No, I do think it still would've happened if the Nina-bot didn't go Skynet. That hate group was around a long time before Bespoke was even a thing. Just because one of them happened to be involved in—

Sure, Cory did notice a lot more abuse, or "hate speech," directed at our Angels, especially in the weeks leading up to... The AI model picked up on all of that too, but after we took it offline, the girls just had to go back to dealing with the abuse on their own. Flagging users, providing negative feedback, even *banning* people.

No. Unfortunately, there was no real way to tell if someone's using a fake email to open an account, 'cause there was no ID used to *create* an account. Credit card information was only taken when users purchased their first tokens. You could always download the app and watch livestreams for free, up to a point.

Look, well over forty-five percent of our users were hiding behind fake emails already. Probably more. So there's no real way to figure out if someone's using a fake email generator to hide their identity, or if they're using their own email but just wanting to keep their identities private.

Sure, there could be kids on the app. It's possible.

Probable even. But it's a double-edged sword, isn't it? We all chant the slogans, the "support sex workers" and "sex work is real work," but when it comes down to it, the right-wing politicians and concerned parents still wanna be in control of what you and I do in our bedrooms. You know goddamn well if it were up to *some* of these people—those "Adam and Eve not Adam and *Steve*" types—Carter and I never would've been allowed to get married.

And now the Supreme Court backed, what— twenty-three states requiring ID for sites and apps like Bespoke? So what did that prove? Did they make the internet any safer for kids?

No, of course they didn't. There's always ways to get around stuff like that. VPNs. Mirror sites. Reddit. Or finding porn in riskier ways, on less regulated, more harmful sites. The dark web or some shit.

So great, you push porn underground, then what? We go back to back-alley abortions, tossing sex workers back on the streets, back to violent pimps and johns? Back to the rampant spread of STIs 'cause the industry's less regulated?

Is that the way?

Or do we *educate*? Do we push parents to be more involved in their children's lives? Do we take the fucking devices out of the kids' hands and go back to the way it was when I was a little latchkey kid in the '80s?

What the fuck do kids need phones for anyway?

But go ahead, blame the internet. Blame social media. Blame the teachers. Blame *porn*.

But don't you fucking *dare* blame the parents.

It couldn't *possibly* be their fault.

Why? Because I'm upset, that's why. You got me riled me up with that fucking... *implication* of yours.

Why are you so fucking interested in all of this, huh? What got you so fired up about Chuck P. and fucking Bespoke in the first place? *Why did you ask me to come here?*

Oh.

Are you—?

Oh, *fuck*.

I'm... I'm so sorry, I didn't even know Tammy had a —she never told—

Of course. Oh, I'm so sorry for your—she was a dear friend, as you know, and I never wanted any of—you have to believe me, what happened wasn't—

No, oh sweetie, please don't cry. Please. Shh. It's okay.

Look, I never... I never wanted any of that to happen. We just wanted, Tammy and me, we wanted to be the best. We wanted to *help* people, you know? Make a... a healthy outlet for people's sexual urges.

We never asked... for *any* of this. Those... *sick scumfucks*... I think they just saw us as an easy target. Fish in a fucking barrel, you know?

But that's what happens when you're at the top. It's like what they say about the tallest blade of grass: it's always the first to get cut.

And sure, those... *fuckers*... they could've gone to Pornhub's headquarters, but they're all the way up in Montreal. They could've hit any of the adult film companies in Porn Valley or Miami or wherever else. But it's mostly office workers there. Executives. Money people.

Bespoke was the only *one-stop-shop*.

We were on the leading edge of the modern porn industry.

And we just so happened to have dozens of performers all in one place. Sixty-eight on that particular day.

And the Nina-bot, yeah. We also had that.

After it happened, after what those maniacs did to... to *my friends*, my colleagues, to *your mother*, those of us left had to make the difficult decision to call—

GAME OVER

It wasn't easy.

I know it should've been, but it wasn't.

This was my *life's work*.

But we did it, we scrapped the app.

Was it inevitable, that turning porn into a game led to a group of pissed-off incel gamers doing what they did to all of those decent, innocent people? You journalists seem to think so, if that's even what you really are. And if you were pretending all this time just to get to this part of my story, then bravo. You had me going. You really should consider getting into real estate. You could sell fucking igloos in Florida.

So what is it you wanna know that I haven't already said a hundred times? You want to hear how they *screamed*? How the gunshots echoing off those high ceilings sounded like fucking *cannon fire* in that big open space? How they looked at me for help... when all I could do was watch them... watch them *die*, and wait for my turn?

You probably saw all the videos, before they scrubbed them. But then, you can never really scrub anything from the internet, can you? Like Candy Rains washing the smell off her hands after the gonorrhea pukefest.

Yeah, you saw it. You watched. I can tell by the look on your face. You know, they said over a million users were viewing at the time, while those sick scumfucks went from pod to pod... shooting one... after another... after another...

Our security? What about it? Look, you must've read all the articles, seen all the news coverage, the police reports. You've done your homework on everything else, I can't imagine you'd drop the ball when it comes to what you *really* came here for.

Yes, our security team was fully trained for firearm use. They were armed guards. We took security very seriously, with the online threats and violent language in the chats, some of the girls even getting harassed out in public or stalked. But let me ask you this: how can *anyone* ever be fully prepared for a *single* active shooter, let alone *three* of them at a time, each one of them trained by *decades* of first-person shooter video games? Anyone but a fucking SWAT team or crisis negotiators or...

I mean, for fuck's sake, look at that school shooting in Texas. Four hundred cops and it took them seventy-something minutes to even do a damn thing. Nineteen kids dead. Two teachers.

Tragedies like that, like what happened at to us at the Power Station, they'd be remarkable if they didn't happen every other goddamn day. You see it on the news and you think, *Those poor people, their poor families*. But you never once expect it could happen to you. To someone you love.

So no, we weren't prepared for what happened. How could we be? Even Mystic Mike and his psychic neighbors network couldn't have predicted that. And if they could, why does it keep happening over and over like a skipping record?

Why do good people keep dying?

Why does evil keep *winning*?

You tell me. I assume you read that kid's manifesto, all that anti-feminist incel bullshit. You saw he cited that massacre in the '80s, the one at the college in Montreal, you know, where the shooter told the men to leave the class, then killed fourteen women and injured a bunch more people before offing himself.

So you know those lunatics were never planning to leave the Power Station alive. They wanted to do a maximum amount of damage until the cops came in and killed them. They *wanted* to be martyrs. He specifically mentioned the seventy-two Angels we had at the Power Station on any given day, said it was like the seventy-two virgins Bin Laden promised the 9/11 terrorists in the afterlife, only with us he said it was "seventy-two sluts."

I dunno if they expected to kill *all* of us, or if they realized how many of our performers were men. I do know they were all using the app regularly, according to the police reports.

You know their names. It turned out we knew them too, or knew *of* them.

Chester Haynes, the one who wrote the CUM Manifesto, who was also the de facto leader of the so-called Control Unity Mastery movement—which most of us jokingly called the

"Celibate Union of Manbabies"—turned out he was one of the worst trolls on the app. He got downvoted enough by our Angels and other users to get kicked off multiple times. He'd just make another fake account and get right back on again. That's what the cops told me anyway. We had no way to find that stuff out. Like I said, probably fifty percent of our users had fake email accounts they used just for the app.

Crying Ugly Masturbators? Yeah, that's a good one too.

The second guy, Reginald Hawksley, he was the violent third in the throuple with our Nina Hollander chatbot. The one that put the other guy in the traction after they danced their hearts out at the Griffith Observatory. After that happened, after he did his twelve-month sentence for aggravated assault, he got right back online. Turns out he created another neural network girlfriend using some online AI app. He was *convinced* the only way to stop obsessing about Nina Hollander was to murder her, and the AI encouraged him. Chatbot psychosis, they call it.

The last one was our disgruntled ex-employee, Max Alden, the IT guy who compromised all our data. Turned out he'd put a previously undetectable back-door app into our security system, allowing them to get into the building undetected through our literal back-door. That's where they bludgeoned Cory to death, who was just out back having a smoke, even though he told me he'd quit two weeks prior.

These scumfucks, they blamed women for all their failures. Blamed their mothers and stepmothers. Alden even blamed his sister for being "hot but unattainable." How fucked up is that? There was literally no personal accountability with any of them. They couldn't get real women because they were "nice guys," according to Chester's thirty-six-page Charles Manson rant. And because they couldn't get laid, they decided to take it out on the world in some anti-feminist power trip.

Where was I when it—? I was in Power Central,

trying not to get shot. The nerve center, yeah, where we kept all the security monitors and Cory's mainframe computers. I tried to get your mom to stay with me, I really did. But of course she wanted to go help the Angels. She died a hero. Whatever you thought about her up to now, your mother died trying to save our friends, while I stayed behind and hid. I'm not proud of that. But what the fuck was I gonna do against three heavily-armed psychos? Try to beat them to death with a fucking dildo?

Your mother... she always was the brave one. I was the brains, she was the guts. She went out there to try and talk the shooters down. I guess you probably saw that. Tried to *negotiate* with them. But like I said, they weren't there to negotiate.

You know what happened to her. You don't need me going over it again.

The cops showed up about thirteen minutes after what those scumfucks did to your mom, and when I tell you it was the longest thirteen minutes of my life, I'm sure you can understand why. The gunshots, the panic, the screaming. Watching my friends die one after another on those fucking security monitors.

I wasn't *just* hiding though. I'm not *that* much of a coward. I was in there trying shut off those fucking streams. I didn't want that shit spread all over the internet. But the backdoor app Max put in, it made sure the streams all stayed running. Wouldn't let me shut them off no matter how hard I tried. They *wanted* people to watch these... *executions*.

That's what they were. Not murders. *Fucking executions*. By the time I realized it wasn't gonna let me shut them off, they'd already shot ten Angels and one of the security guards on shift, Paul Cronin.

Then I realized, if I shut off the power, it'd cut the feeds off at the source. I hoped it'd fuck with those maniacs, not being able to see. But I guess they were counting on the cops cutting the power, 'cause the fucks brought night vision goggles.

Everyone after that, they killed in the dark. I couldn't see any of it with the lights out and all the monitors shut off. Just the muzzle flashes in one pod after another, snatches of frantic movement inside. I didn't have to imagine how they felt, 'cause I was right there with them, watching the door, waiting for it to burst open and *BANG!*

Lights out for me too.

When the cops finally came in—*stormed* in, I should say—I guess they heard the shots fired and figured there wasn't any time for negotiations. They just started blasting away. The whole shootout lasted... maybe five minutes. They killed both Hawksley and Alden, but Haynes, the one who orchestrated the whole thing, it turned out he was a bigger coward than his buddies. He gave himself up.

By then, there were twenty-six dead. Nineteen injured.

Twenty-two of the victims, the ones who died there or later, in the hospital, they were women. Your mother, Nina Hollander, the Wholesome Twins, Jeri and Dawn. I could name them all, but what'd be the point? It's not like you knew any of the others. And it's not like naming them's gonna stop me from seeing their last moments every time I close my fucking eyes.

The four men? Cory, Horace the Human Dildo, and the two guards, Ed Ashworth and Paul Cronin. Paul just had a little baby girl two weeks prior. I heard they named her Tammy, not that that's any consolation to you.

That's not counting those scumfucks Hawksley and Alden, of course.

Haynes, he's serving a life sentence without parole barely a twenty-minute drive from here, in Wende Correctional.

No, I never visited him. I tried. They have a no-contact policy for victims, without special approval from the warden. I could try to get that, if I wanted. But what'd be the point? I said all I needed to say at his trial.

You could, if you wanted.

Hell, you probably *should*.

Carter? How did he feel about all this? Well, he left me, if that tells you anything. We had a rough go of it for a while there, trying to keep things amicable. But he... after six or seven months of trying, he told me he couldn't live with the man I'd become any longer.

No, he's a sweetheart. We're still close. And I don't blame him in the least for leaving. 'Cause he was right, I am different now. Cynical. Angry. Scared *all the fucking time*. Carter did what he could to help me, but I need to help myself. I have to drag myself out of this hell I created.

You *pivot*. That's right.

I guess that's why I decided to do this interview with you, or whatever this really is. An intervention, I guess you could call it. I guess it turned out to be something of a tear-soaked confessional after all, didn't it? But that's probably why I avoided interviews for... almost a year. I wasn't ready.

Then you called, and something just clicked. That's why I said yes.

Maybe it was fate.

Maybe it was your mom, telling me to do it from the Great Beyond. I think she'd have liked that explanation.

Or maybe... maybe it was the Lonely Motel, calling me home. Back to where it all started.

So do I believe in curses? I don't know. Feels like I've been cursed as much as I've been blessed. Tragedy and triumph, and all that.

What do *you* think? Do *you* believe?

No, I guess maybe I don't either. But you *feel* different now, don't you? Like you've changed?

I told you. *You can't leave this place unchanged.*

There's *always* a toll. Always a *price*. You might pay it now, or you might pay it later.

What's next for me? You mean with my life?

I don't know. I've thought about it a lot. Had a lot of time since we closed up shop at the Power Station, to think on things.

At first I thought I'd go back to my roots. Try writing and directing a *real* movie. A horror film. There's a lot of money in horror these days, and why wouldn't there be? *Something's* gotta distract us from all the *real* horror going on out there, day to day.

But if I'm honest? I think it might be time to hang up my hat. You know, retire. I've had more than my share of triumphs and tragedies for one lifetime.

Fuck this town. Fuck this country! I should be sipping Panty Rippers on some beach in Belize, not freezing my nuts off in these frigid fucking winters.

But we'll see. I'll tell you one thing I *do* know for sure: the Lonely Motel was where I got my start, but I am never coming back to this fucking place again.

Hand on heart.

ACKNOWLEDGMENTS

Like the previous book in the Lonely Motel series, I've been wanting to tell this story for quite some time. I just didn't know how to get started with it. CVLT (Book 3) was sitting unfinished on my computer since 2018 or so. This one was just in my notes, and my head.

I knew I wanted to tell this one a little differently. All of the Lonely Motel books are about people telling stories. In Woom, it was two people in a motel room baring their traumas. In *Gross Out*, it was a ton of writers at a horror convention. In *CVLT*, it was back to two people in a motel room, this time battling wits.

For *Shoot* (whose working title was *Fuck*, but with an asterisk so I could get away with it), I wanted to try something different. I've done a few monologues before, but nothing longer than a short story. Since they were all about people telling stories, I thought it would be fun to have Chuck Power tell his story directly to the reader. But I couldn't figure out a way to do that until recently.

Once I decided it would be essentially a dramatic monologue, told to a journalist, the story poured out of me like... well, you just read the book. You can pick and choose the various ways it might have poured out of me, metaphorically speaking.

I had a ton of fun writing it. And it became a helluva lot darker than how it started. Mystic Mike, for instance, was never a part of my original story notes.

Nor was the Control Unity Mastery movement and their manifesto.

As always, I hope you enjoyed reading it, and if you wouldn't mind popping up a review/rating wherever you purchased it, I'd be ever so grateful. These Lonely Motel books are a labor of love, and if you'd like more of them (and I plan to write more), the chances they'll be written sooner are higher the more word of mouth these books get.

———

Thanks to everyone in my ARC reader group for early reading and catching errors. Any remaining proofing issues are the responsibility of the author. Extra thanks to Andrew Adams (author of *Son of a Serial Killer*) and Daniel Nobles for catching more errors than I could have without their eyes.

That's all for now. As I said last time, I've got at least one or two more books in the works for it (including Shyla and Angel's last dance, so to peak), and I'm super excited for what's to come.

I hope you'll continue on this journey with me. Your room is waiting....

D.R.
October, 2025

About the Author

Author of the cult smash-hit *Woom* and *Ghostland* and more than 15 other books that aren't the cult smash-hit *Woom* or *Ghostland*. His debut collection was blurbed positively by the legendary Jack Ketchum. His novel, *Pedo Island Bloodbath*, was nominated for a 2024 Splatterpunk Award for Best Novel.

For 10 *free* dark fiction short stories/novellas including the prequel to *GHOSTLAND*, "The Moving House," signed copies of Woom, bookplates and merch, please visit www.duncanralston.com.

For more delicious dark fiction,

visit **www.duncanralston.com**

and **www.shadowworkpublishing.com.**